FINDING HUMOR IN GRIEF

By

Dr. Ruth L. Baskerville

ISBN-13: 978-1522814023

ISBN-10: 1522814027

Published by:
Dr. Ruth L. Baskerville

Cover Design by:
R. Bruce Lankford

Table of Contents

Dedication

Naturally, this book is dedicated to my dear husband of nearly half a century, Waverly Lee Baskerville, Jr. He is the main character of the story, around which so many persons who adored and respected him revolve. I didn't think I could love him in death more than I did when he was with me, but as I reflect daily on our enduring relationship, I'm convinced that we experienced life's adventures as one body.

Yes, I kept playful secrets from him, thus ensuring the longevity of our marriage. However, there was nothing substantive, whether wonderful or terrible, that Waverly and I didn't share. Early in our marriage, we vowed never to end a day upset with each other, and we kept that promise.

I also want to dedicate this book to my daughter, Alicia Lankford. Whenever my stress point over losing Waverly increased, her ability to handle tough situations grew stronger. As often as I needed to see her or hear her voice to comfort me, I found her. I'm amazed and impressed with the woman of faith and mother Alicia has become.

In my first book, which I dedicated to Waverly, I recalled the song that says, *"If you get the chance to sit it out or dance, DANCE!"* The love and courage imparted to me by my "Darling Forever" sustain me, enabling me to dance for as long as God allows me to breathe.

Introduction

My husband, Waverly Lee Baskerville, Jr. died on March 13, 2012. We had been married for almost forty-five years, which meant that I had not just lost the company of my one true love, but I was also lost! We were each other's best friends for our entire adult lives. Whatever one of us thought to do was filtered through the lens of what we knew about the other's desires.

I thought it impossible to survive without him because there were too many tasks, decisions, plans that he alone managed. Dividing responsibilities is typical in long-term relationships, and couples are *supposed* to view each other as if the union will remain "awhile longer," if not "forever."

As I shared with family and close friends my struggle to accomplish a myriad of left-brain tasks previously foreign to me, they laughed heartily. They called my stories "hilarious," though my retort was, *"I don't see what's so funny!"*

I saw that grief *did* have a funny side, and the title of my book came to me: ***FINDING HUMOR IN GRIEF.***

Each segment tells a different aspect of my journey to successfully function without Waverly. I reveal my intimate thoughts and actions in a stream-of-conscience writing style, rather than to tell my story in chronological order. I don't think anyone will be confused.

Most experiences I recount are highly amusing to all readers, but for those times when I found no humor, I created a chapter called *"Mama Said There'd Be Days Like This."* Writing this book was cathartic for me, but I also wanted to connect with readers who are mourning like I am. Humor is excellent medicine for the ailing mind, body and soul.

I apologized to a dear friend for naively thinking that grieving over the loss of her husband was something that diminished in time. I foolishly likened her grief to a wound that looked awfully painful at first, but got better each day until only a tiny scar remained. I now know that these distinct scars will never disappear, and that coping with grief is the only way to find a measure of happiness again. It's called a "new normal."

I've learned that grief is like a roller coaster, where the ride never ends, and the goal is to find the courage to let go your grip of the safety bar and raise your arms high in the air, as you "free fall" with confidence that you'll land safely, in your right mind.

Chapter One
The Death of an Exceptional Man

Waverly Lee Baskerville, Jr., age sixty-four, passed away on March 13, 2012. The day before his Home Going Celebration service, I sat at the computer and without pausing, wrote this tribute to my beloved husband:

"Darling, Forever"
by Dr. Ruth L. Baskerville
Home Going Celebration, March 18, 2012

"I saw this handsome, skinny soccer player walk across the college campus, and immediately fell in love. I heard those bells and whistles people talk of, and I knew I had to have this man for my lifetime partner. We married while still in college, had baby Alicia, and graduated with two diplomas and a healthy one-year old child. We drove to Waverly's parents' home in Newark, NJ with eighty-seven cents in our pockets and no milk for baby Alicia. That was our beginning.

My father gave us a family Bible, in which he wrote that we were "The Happiness Kids" because we were so in love and so happy. Our home décor went from black lights and hanging beads between rooms, to a water bed with mirrors on the canopy, to the delicate balance between my love of silver and fine china, and Waverly's love of Black pilots and cowboys, with enough leather horses to fill a small stable.

While looking at family pictures to choose the best for a memorial collage, I saw that he sported the Afro look and the bald look, wore the bathing suit and the barbecue shorts, presented himself in business suits and a black-tie tuxedo. We had a full life!

Our first apartment contained less than a dozen pieces of furniture, none of them new. One day, Waverly came home with a picture of a red Corvette, which he taped to the empty wall. I called him a "dreamer," saying we would never have such wealth. But he had the determination and work ethic to make me a dreamer, too. We later owned that red Corvette and many more top model vehicles after that.

Along our journey, Waverly insisted that we reach back and mentor young people seeking a better life. He was a role model in the neighborhood and on the job. He was as generous a man to family and friends as he was to himself. He took quiet pleasure in seeing others happy and productive.

Many people knew that Waverly was a private, cautious man who was married to an adventurous woman. Few knew that the reason I soared before learning how to flap my wings was that I always had Waverly to catch me. He was a strong

1

taskmaster, pushing my career forward when I preferred to stay in my comfort zone. But each time I followed his lead, I did more, I had more, I WAS more.

When we married at nineteen years old, while still in college, I was uncertain of our future. Waverly wasn't. He knew that we were meant to be life partners. Recently, I told him how exciting my life had been these past forty-four years because he kept things fresh and full of surprises. He responded by saying that it was I who added the forty-four years of suspense that we shared, as well.

Waverly was my life partner, my friend, my lover, my mentor. I can't imagine sleeping in the bed without him or eating a meal without having light conversation with him. I retired last spring, and we had the gift of time together, day and night, for almost a year. God needed him before I was ready to give him up, so I accept God's will.

He used to sign the cards he gave me with the words, 'Darling, Forever,' so I'll end my tribute to the most remarkable man I'll ever know, with this: 'Waverly, Dear, You'll be proud watching me continue to soar, this time reading the manual for wing span dimensions, and remembering the lessons you taught me. I'll be fine until we meet again.' Your Darling, Forever, Ruthie."

There you have it! I was among the luckiest women on earth to have met my one true love and soul mate at the tender age of nineteen, and with whom I was blessed to build an extraordinary life. For all the years Waverly was a corporate tax specialist on Wall Street, he commuted from New Jersey to New York by train. Every night when I picked him up at the local train station, my heart fluttered with the same girlish passion as the first time we met. We were lovers and best friends who never lost the fervor that began our relationship.

Waverly was diabetic and he had heart surgery six years before he died. He experienced trouble sleeping and breathing during the holidays in 2011, and he shared his concern with his cardiologist at his annual checkup. The doctor asked to see him every week for two months, adjusting medicine after each blood test.

Waverly's gait gradually slowed, to the point that he stood behind me and walked holding onto my shoulders. We were convinced that whatever was wrong, Waverly and Ruthie could fix it, once doctors found the problem and prescribed the remedy.

During the time in which he had weekly cardiologist visits and weekly blood tests, he also saw his primary physician, who found "no visual field loss, no diplopia, no blurry vision, no cough, no hemoptysis, no wheezing, no heartburn, no nausea, no abdominal pain, no speech difficulties, and no sensory disturbances."

Waverly also saw his endocrinologist, who was proud enough of his blood level readings to say she would consider reducing his medication at the next visit in six months. Waverly took so many blood tests for the three doctors that I was certain he would run out of blood if a diagnosis weren't found quickly.

Just nine days before he died, Waverly had asked me to call "911" to send an ambulance to take him to the hospital. Although we had been visiting his cardiologist weekly for seven weeks, he wasn't getting better. So we were scheduled to see a kidney and a lung specialist soon. But he felt he couldn't wait for those appointments.

Since he had never made an urgent request of me before, I immediately made the call, and within less than an hour, we were in the hospital emergency room. They determined that his sodium was dangerously low, and he was admitted. During the six days before he was released, they monitored every vital sign. When we left the hospital that Sunday evening, we had instructions to see a couple of new doctors. On Monday, I set the appointments, the first of which was Tuesday morning with the doctor in whose office Waverly collapsed.

As he rounded the receptionist's desk to enter the exam room, he collapsed without warning. He sank to the floor like a rag doll, making no grimace or sound to suggest he was in pain. The doctor's assistant and I cradled Waverly's head as he fell, bending our bodies to follow him to the floor. The doctor immediately started CPR, while calling the paramedics to say that he wasn't breathing. They arrived shortly, since the hospital was nearby.

As they worked to revive him, I called my daughter, Alicia, and announced through uncontrollable sobbing, *"Daddy's not breathing!"* Within half an hour, she had loaded her four children into the car and sped to the hospital to meet me. She called her husband, Bruce, who joined us shortly thereafter. By the time they arrived, my Waverly was gone forever.

I followed the ambulance that took him to the emergency room. When I entered the hospital a week earlier, I had to wait, show identification, and be escorted to his treatment area. This time, a Spiritual Care Chaplain met me and insisted that I come with her immediately. My stomach was knotted, tears stinging the back of my eyes as I made it into her quiet, little room. My body trembled when I looked into her eyes.

I burst into tears after hearing that the paramedics were unable to get Waverly's heart started. I needed to see him right away! My heart was racing and my face was red and hot. My head started pounding, almost blinding my vision. I was breathless and incoherent, as I tried unsuccessfully to get control of myself.

Waverly was lying on a bed in a private area with curtains drawn around him. Aside from the tube in his mouth, he looked like he was peacefully resting. His body had swelled from medics' attempts to push air into his lungs. I felt despair, unable to do a thing to help him or me. I heard my daughter's voice on the other side of the curtain, as the Chaplain offered to watch the children while she came into the private area with her Daddy and me.

We cried hard. Neither of us could console the other. He had been in the constant care of doctors for weeks, and taken more tests in two months than he had in two years previously. What did they miss? What did I miss? What happened? Was it his time to die, according to God's plan? Could I have done anything differently to keep him alive?

Piling unanswered, probably unanswerable questions on top of one another did nothing to assuage our sadness. We needed to get control of this terrible situation, but how?

I remembered to tell the physician on call that Waverly was an organ and tissue donor, and that he wished to be cremated. Someone would call me later that day. Alicia described the whole thing as "surreal." I felt outrage and hopelessness at the same time.

My legs trembled as I left the hospital without my "Darling Forever." I was frightened, anxious and confused about what to do first. I wasn't ready to stop crying, so I didn't even try. I wondered where my God was in all of this, but I repeated out loud the words I had so often used to comfort others: *"God never makes mistakes, so we must rely on faith to understand His actions."*

Alicia drove me home, as I cried out loud and used up the small pack of tissues given me by the Spiritual Care Chaplain. Alicia used up all her tissues, too. Bruce and the kids followed us. Everyone was crying. We had to tell the sad news to my whole family and all our friends. We had to plan a funeral, and I had to figure out how to live without Waverly. We hadn't spent more than a week apart during each decade of our marriage.

The next hours were a daze for me. There were decisions that I suddenly had to make, and I couldn't get my mind to focus. My daughter took my phone book and contacted all the relatives, our friends and neighbors in several states. It was Alicia who told the shocking news, and who comforted those crying on the other end of the phone. She absorbed everyone else's pain and loss, while finding the quiet strength to stay composed. Perhaps that was her way of dealing with her own sadness and loss, but I just couldn't make the calls.

My three Florida siblings arrived to my home within the hour, immediately handling funeral arrangements for me. Waverly died on Tuesday, and the "Home Going Celebration" would be the following Sunday afternoon. My brother in New York was on the way, as were my best friends from college. I wanted the service to be at our home.

My brothers and sisters planned every detail, from ordering food to placing chairs under a large canopy in the back yard. My sister-in-law decorated the whole yard beautifully, and my son-in-law set up a sophisticated sound system for the service over which his Dad, Bishop Richard would preside. He and his wife, and Bruce's sister and family were coming from Atlanta.

While we were discussing the funeral, the folks from The Organ and Tissue Donation Institute contacted me to take the necessary steps for Waverly's organ donation. The funeral parlor handling cremation wanted me to select an urn for Waverly's ashes. My mind shifted to my own death, since I'm also an organ and tissue donor who wants to be cremated. Could arrangements really be made this quickly, this efficiently? Wasn't I forgetting something important?

My first best friend arrived at midnight without luggage, and designed the Home Going Program before attempting to have her suitcase shipped to my home. Waverly's Dad, whom we all called "Pop," was almost ninety years old. He found it incredulous that his namesake died before him.

He couldn't make the journey, so Waverly's baby brother stayed with him. They chose a song and *HOLY BIBLE* verse to include in the service. Every conversation about the service ended with all of us crying. Still we planned purposefully. Flowers, cards and food baskets arrived in large numbers. The phone rang constantly. There were moments where I felt the world spinning around me, as if I were looking at the scene as an outsider. Other moments captured all of my raw emotions.

My first humorous remembrance of those horrible events was of Alicia and I picking up the brown and gold urn from the funeral parlor. They had made a special effort to have it ready before the Home Going Celebration, so that we wouldn't be addressing an empty urn during the program.

It was heavier than I imagined, and Alicia held it while I drove home. Before we got out of the car, she asked if we should look inside the urn to see the ashes. *"I think they seal these things,"* I said. She replied, *"I don't think so, Mommy, because many people scatter their loved-one's ashes in a particular place that was dear to the deceased person."*

I gently loosened the top of the urn, and sure enough, it opened easily to reveal a plastic bag in which was a white substance that looked like a cross between sugar and flour. It was pure white! I couldn't help but remark, *"You know, dear, your father was a proud Black man all his life, and now he's reduced to a pure white powder. Daddy would NOT be pleased!"*

On the morning of the Home Going Celebration, the house was full of overnight guests and local family members. Folks had been working since sunrise to ready the backyard for the service. Everyone except me was hungry. One of my dearest friends pulled breakfast stuff from the refrigerator and cooked. All the workers piled into the kitchen, sitting or standing as we prayed before sharing our first meal of the day.

The only time I was completely alone was when I showered. I cried out loud while the water ran, and then looked at my gradually swelling eyes in the mirror. When I appeared downstairs, dressed in black, my family was checking the order of the program and the technology that would bring Pop and Brother Phil Baskerville's voices to us from New Jersey. We were ready for the Home Going Celebration. I noticed that the sky was clear on that bright, sunny Sunday morning with a slight breeze blowing.

Friends and colleagues from the school in Georgia where I had my last principal's assignment drove through the night to be with me. Floral arrangements and plants, fruit and cheese baskets, candy and food were both inside the house and on the tastefully decorated lanai. I was surrounded by an abundance of loving people, but had no privacy, which might have been a good thing.

I grabbed Alicia's hand, and we entered the lanai after everyone was seated, while spiritually uplifting music was playing. We took our seats, so far composed. I felt my older brother's strong hand squeeze my shoulder as I sat in front of him. I choked up, but did not cry yet.

Chapter Two
Humor at the Home Going Celebration
"What's so funny, Lucy?"

The service began promptly at 2:00 p.m., the way Waverly would have wanted it. A fairly new friend, Rev. Michael gave the Invocation. My daughter, Alicia spoke with the voice of an Angel, and I followed, reading my piece, "Darling Forever." I managed to read it without crying, but as I looked up from my paper, nearly everyone else was reaching for tissues and softly weeping.

We heard Waverly's baby brother sing a tribute to his big brother, and we heard Pop read two Psalms chapters with the clarity that made us feel as if they were present, instead of eight states away. Technology is a wonderful thing!

Bishop Richard captured the essence of a complicated man. He said, *"Waverly was the kind of person who made you straighten up your attire and stand at attention when he came into the room. He set the highest standard for everyone he met, his own life an example of reaching for nothing less than the top at work and at home."* Every word Bishop Richard said wasn't glowing, but it was accurate.

He then asked if persons wanted to speak, and my baby sister took the microphone. She paid a serious and humorous tribute to her brother-in-law, including these words that evoked laughter from the attendees:☐

"I remember when I used to spend the summer with Ruthie and Waverly, and I babysat for two-year-old Alicia. Ruthie was ironing and trying to be thrifty back then, so she would press and starch Waverly's shirts instead of sending them to the dry cleaners. She would say, 'He doesn't know the difference,' as she carefully folded each shirt around the cardboard backing and inserted it into the plastic cover. The next night, Waverly told me how much he appreciated and loved his wife. 'She even presses and starches my shirts to save money, and she doesn't think I know she's not going to the cleaners.'

I also remember when Ruthie taught high school drama. As Waverly sat proudly in the audience watching her production, he would

notice the expensive items on the stage that she had 'borrowed' from their home to use as props. He was obviously also a very patient man!"

Next, both my brothers spoke tenderly about their love and respect for Waverly, along with their appreciation for his special treatment of their sister. My nephew wrote a poem about this remarkable man who gave him good advice as a young man. My Georgia friends paid public tribute to Waverly's guidance and protection of his beloved wife. My good friend shared the way she learned that my husband was the same person she knew back in high school, and how they were reunited.

As the service ended, neighbors and family members organized serving lines for food and drink. The atmosphere turned from somber to quietly comfortable, as everyone got acquainted. They took turns checking to see how I was doing, whether or not I was eating, if I were crying and needed comfort.

Bits of conversations floated past me, as I reflected on the elegant tribute to my dear Waverly. Folks passed by the urn containing his ashes, and then focused on the large collage of pictures depicting a life lived well. Many guests saw pictures of themselves in the collage.

My other sister was laughing with those sitting near her, as she embellished on my drama days as a high school English teacher.

"One Saturday morning, Waverly went to the local post office and saw a large poster announcing Ruth's latest production. There at the bottom was THEIR unlisted phone number to call for tickets. When he got home, he asked why his unlisted phone number was displayed on the town's post office door. 'How else will folks know where to get tickets, Honey?' was my sister's reply." I was again crying softly, but had to pause to laugh at myself for that one!

I joined in the conversation. *"Then there was the time I needed Waverly's silk smoking jacket for a play, and when he arrived at the production, having come straight from work with no dinner, he quietly said through tight lips, 'Lucy, is that boy wearing my silk jacket?'*

He called me 'Lucy' instead of 'Ruthie' on occasion. Whenever I came home and said, 'Honey, you'll never believe what just happened to me,' his response, without looking up from whatever he was doing, was always, 'Sure I would, LUCY!' That's enough about my theatre tales!"

I walked over to another cluster of people gathering around my baby sister, who insisted that I tell everyone how Waverly *became* an organ donor. Reluctantly, I shared the true story:

"Fifteen years ago, I had gotten three speeding tickets in a row and had my license taken away for thirty days. All the women here know that the secret to a long and happy marriage is to tell our men things on a 'need to know basis.' Waverly didn't need to know that, if I could solve the problem without having to tell him.

I called the sister who most resembled me, asking her to pretend to lose her license and get a replacement. She would then send me the 'lost' license for thirty days, and I'd return it when I got mine back. It was a great plan, and she, of course, complied without saying anything to end her happy marriage. She got a new license and mailed hers to me the next day.

When it arrived, I laughed at the fact that I would now be eight years younger, with a perfect driving record. I stopped laughing when I saw that she was an organ donor. I told her that if I got into an accident and Waverly found out what I had done, he would personally take my organs and donate them before burying me. I was a perfect driver for those thirty days, and did, in fact, get my license back. I mailed my sister's license back to her, but then felt guilty about the organ donor thing.

So I promised God that I would become an organ donor when I renewed my license. Since Waverly and I did everything together, he said, 'Honey, I think it's a great idea for us to become organ donors. I never thought about it before.' He and I became organ and tissue donors that day. Well, he died first, and so he became a donor before me."

The group that had gathered to hear my story laughed loudly, and I joined in. My sister chuckled, *"He never knew the truth,"* to which someone else responded while looking towards Heaven, *"He might know it NOW!"*

My sisters had become most talkative by this point, probably because the audience had grown! In retrospect, I think everyone needed some comic relief in order to deal with our great and unexpected loss.

"Remember the last time we three sisters had our annual end-year 'Girls Night Out' at Ruth's timeshare? We always spent the first afternoon in the pool and hot tub, followed by excessive eating and drinking, and making predictions about what the following year would bring each of us. We stayed up late sharing childhood memories, and had breakfast together before returning to our respective homes.

Ruth had a habit of putting her cell phone in her bra for easy access when it rang. When she put her bathing suit on, she must have tucked the phone in there before getting into the pool." All eyes were on me, as I finished that story at my own expense.

"I felt a buzzing, like a small electric chair was somewhere near me. We realized together that it was my phone, and I quickly retrieved it and wrapped it in a towel. Too late! The phone was vibrating, and moving by itself all around the towel, as if possessed by jumping beans. We tried to blow dry the little computer chip inside with a hair dryer. No use. It was ruined. How could I explain this to Waverly? Simple! I wouldn't!!

On my way home from our overnight splendor, I found a Sprint store and insisted that I needed an exact duplicate of my red cell phone. When the store clerk expressed sadness at the fact that I had lost everything stored in the ruined phone, I assured him that I had lost nothing, but did need the same phone number. Luckily, I was technologically challenged, so there was nothing in the memory except the last thirty calls. That was easy.

Before going home, I rubbed the shiny new phone against the pavement a few times to give it the character that comes from having been used more than five years. It looked a bit more worn than I anticipated, with all the shine gone from the outer casing. Oh, well, it was better than my bringing home a bright red phone that Waverly would instantly know was new!

So when he asked how I enjoyed my sisters, I replied that we had a great time bonding together, as always. In truth, our bond was, 'This is another of Ruthie's secrets that we'll take to our graves.' I believe we fooled Waverly one more time. How else could I have reached forty-four successful years of marriage?"

Someone commented on how rare it is today for couples to stay married that long. They asked for my secret. *"When people ask me the secret to a happy, long marriage, I tell them this: Always remember that we women are but a rib of man. I used that logic with Waverly dozens of times, and it always empowered him. I usually got what I wanted because I had mastered the art of being a subservient wife. That's the secret to a happy marriage — manipulation of a whole body by a mere rib!!"*

Without warning, the mood became solemn and quiet. Some folks went to the food table for desserts and coffee. I excused myself and found a quiet place near the pool to sit and ponder the days' events. I felt tears coming on, and drank a big glass of water to hold them back.

It was only five days since I last saw Waverly alive. What ever would I do without him? How was I supposed to move forward? What would I do when all my friends and relatives returned to their lives and I was alone with my thoughts? Tears rolled down my cheeks onto my chin before I found a dinner napkin to wipe my face.

Little Sister sensed the change in my state of mind, and she sat right next to me with a comforting arm across my back. She said, *"Waverly was my brother and I loved him. Although I can't see him, I can still speak to him. And one day, I will see him again, and this gives me great comfort, as I hope it does you.*

I read a book by Susan Hunt that said, 'The mysterious and marvelous mercy of God has convinced me of one thing - it is dark because I am in that deep, hidden place under God's wing.' God has you gently tucked under His wing right now, Ruthie." She kissed and hugged me, after which I excused myself to go inside and wash my face. I knew that my eyes were red and swollen again.

As I left the area, I heard my former assistant principal, now a principal: *"Waverly was like family to my wife and me. He helped me find perspective and strength during some dark days in my career. I followed his advice and always came out on top. He will always have a place in our hearts. Alexis and I thought so highly of him, and we truly miss him."*

A neighbor referred to him as "Neighborly Waverly" because he was always watching over the homes on our street. He knew what car everyone drove, what time neighbors came and went, and looked out for suspicious vehicles, which appeared on rare occasions. I smiled as I heard many other testimonials from friends and relatives. Still, I wanted to be alone, just for a little while.

My family began moving food from the lanai to the kitchen, as folks began leaving. My brother kissed me gently and said, *"My dear brother-in-law has loved my sister so very much over these past forty-four years and I will always love him for that. He and you, Ruthie, raised a beautiful daughter whom I am very proud of. Waverly made you both strong, and he WILL see you again. What a blessing that I had him in my life all these years! He was an inspiration to me, and he'll be missed until we meet again."*

One of my former educational colleagues said, as she fought back tears, *"My dear Dr. B., you and your family are constantly in my prayers. Waverly was such a strong man who would do anything to protect his family. We will surely see him again. He's in Heaven smiling down on us all. Remember, God always picks the prettiest flower first."* She and my other Georgia friends had to leave to drive all night, in order to be back at work the next day. I appreciated immensely their sacrifice of time and sleep, just to be with me for a few hours.

One by one, everyone left except my best friends who stayed the night. The house became quiet again, and I wished I could hold Waverly or talk to him just one more time. Folks handled the cleanup and taking down the decorations. Someone placed a cup of fresh, hot coffee in front of me, and I drank it, lost in thought.

Two of the male relatives placed the ceramic urn with Waverly's remains on a high shelf in the room that greets the sun every morning. I could see it each morning from the kitchen, and I liked that. I don't know if I'll ever scatter the ashes over some place that was special to him, but for now, I'm able to greet Waverly as I start each day. I draw huge comfort from keeping him close to me. I'm so happy to have received information that a stranger received sight from his corneas. His bones also gave life to someone I'll never know. It's all good!

Chapter Three
Security and Repairs
Home Sweet Home

Waverly was a stickler for maintaining home security. He always put the house alarm on, even when we drove to a store five minutes away and would be gone half an hour. If we walked our dog, Lucky, we armed the house first. I used to criticize him for being overly cautious, considering the fact that we lived in a good neighborhood and had never had an attempted break-in. His reply was consistent. *"There's always a first time, and I'd rather be careful than robbed."*

After Waverly died, I had to force myself to check my purse for my house keys every time I went out. I never used to worry about having my keys because he always had his. It was fear of being locked out of my house that made me remember to carry my keys everywhere, and give the second set to my daughter. I also learned to check that all exterior doors were locked before I put the alarm on and exited my home. That was relatively painless!

However, one night, I let Lucky out for her last pee before bed, and something caught her eye. She moved out of my view, so I stepped outside and walked a little distance until I could see her. Just then, a breeze blew the front door shut.

I knew I had done a good job locking all doors for the evening, and no, I didn't carry my house keys in my pajamas because when would I have occasion to need them? I had no pockets, either! There I stood in my nightclothes, as Lucky playfully returned to the front door glancing at me as if I had lost my senses by not opening the door for us right away.

My phones were in the house, too, so I had to cross the street in my pajamas and wake a neighbor to use the phone to wake my daughter to drive half an hour to let me into my home. All this time, Lucky gave me the look I imagine Waverly would have given if he were still alive. That was a "Lucy" maneuver, but it was the last time I would open my front door without taking the lock off. Since then, Lucky has disappeared from my sight half a dozen times, but *not once* did the wind blow my *unlocked* front door shut behind me!

We have an intercom system throughout the house, which also provides radio station access and a wakeup call to your favorite radio sound. I never used the intercom. I pressed one button to play music on the radio. I never used the wake up call system because I had a modest alarm clock that I set nightly. It was Waverly who gently awakened houseguests with his announcement that breakfast was served. It was Waverly who delighted me early Sunday mornings with Gospel music throughout the house.

After he passed away, I inadvertently set the alarm on the intercom system, thinking I was changing the radio station. In the middle of the night, I jumped up from a deep sleep to hear loud Rap music permeating every space in my home. I thought an intruder was inside, intending to do me harm. Perhaps he intended to "Rap" me to death before robbing me!

I knew that Waverly's extensive gun collection was across the hallway in his office, so I ran in the dark, half naked, from my bedroom to the office. I fumbled for the light switch, raced to unlock the drawer with guns and ammunition, and then bit my lip because I had no idea what bullets belonged to which guns. Nor did I know how to load even the little pistol.

As my heart raced and my head pounded, I vacillated between holding a big gun that *looked* loaded, or brandishing one of Waverly's Japanese swords in front of the intruder to scare him away. And why did I leave the bedroom wearing only panties and his undershirt? The bad guy could be a rapper, a thief and a rapist!

The music seemed louder, more intense, which I suddenly realized was due to the fact that I was standing next to the intercom button in the office. Oh! There was no intruder, but instead I was receiving a wakeup call at 2:45 a.m. – to Rap music, no less!

I put my weapons down and gave my full attention to turning off the music and unsetting the alarm. I accomplished the first task in one minute, and the second in two days.

I now know how to get Sunday morning Gospel all over the house, but my next overnight guest will hear me yell from the bottom of the staircase, *"Breakfast is ready!!"*

Over the Christmas holidays, my first as a widow, I had two major expenses in a row. Neither fit neatly into my widow's budget, which I called my "austerity retirement plan." I was entertaining some lovely ladies from the Simply Sisters Spiritual Women's Organization to which I belonged, and both downstairs toilets overflowed before dessert. I was mortified. This had never happened before! The guests traveled to the upstairs bathrooms, which worked fine.

The next morning, I asked my neighbor if he knew of a plumber, but my description of the problem told him I needed a septic service.

"When was the last time you had the tank emptied?" Never! No one told us we had to do that. We assumed that putting Rid-X into a toilet monthly released enzymes that devoured everything. Right? That's what it says on the label of the bottle.

"My dear, your overflowing toilets on the first floor are telling you to get your septic tank emptied, or you will have you know what all over your yard in due time." I was stunned. Up North, we never had well water or septic tanks, so how would I know what care they needed? I definitely comprehended the meaning of *"you know what all over your yard"* though!

I called the recommended company, and the first person who came wanted me to personally see how deep the tank was and how much he had to dig to get to it. He must have thought I recognized at once that my tank was larger and buried deeper than the normal septic tank. My focus was on the big patch of grass he had pulled up to get to the tank. It ruined my manicured lawn!

After making a few indistinguishable groans, the nice man said that I first had to fix two broken pipes, then do some electrical work, and finally empty the tank. I heard myself say something I remember hearing as a child, but that I never said in my adult life: *"Does your company take post-dated checks?"* They did, because it was Christmastime, and because they saw fear in my eyes. When I saw the bill for my "oversized" tank, my fear turned to silent rage.

Before I could catch my breath from that inconvenient expense, the home security system stopped working. Turned out that, due to the holidays, no one could come out for two days. I could still lock all the doors, but should an intruder *know* that a break-in wouldn't bring the police to my door, or that I possessed unloaded guns with tons of ammunition lying beside them, he could pillage and plunder without fear. I told my little Schnoodle, Lucky to use her killer bark for the next two days, but anyone gazing at the gold and red holiday bow on her sparkling collar might surmise that she was no threat.

I made it through two days without security and without incidents. The alarm guy said all my windows had shorted out and had no alarm capacity. The doors were OK. I needed new units on all the windows. He assured me that he could have everything fixed within three hours, which was handy because I had dinner guests coming in two hours.

Just as he told me not to move because I would disturb the newly installed motion detector and bring the police or fire vehicles, the doorbell rang. I instinctively moved to answer it. That triggered the alarm, and the police were on their way.

All my friends wanted was a quiet dinner, without a police search.

Luckily, the alarm guy got through to cancel the police while they were en route. He gave me the bill and left. Dinner was uneventful after that.

I was now the proud owner of brand new alarm equipment and a septic tank capable of one million flushes before I could expect the first sign of trouble. If an intruder came here that night, I would have asked, with an attitude, *"What did you bring me?"*

Chapter Four
Maintaining the Pool
Saying Goodbye to Waverly's World

I was doing pretty well by the time Waverly had been gone seven months. I cried about every other day. Usually, I'd be driving somewhere and notice tears on my neck, before I realized they had left my eyes and rolled down my cheeks. Coming home to an empty house was hard, so I used writing in my journal as my therapy. It helped!

I left my pain on the page and was able to do productive things instead of crying for long periods of time and questioning God's plan. I had no doubt that God had a plan. He just didn't share it with me because He knew I'd put a comma where He put a period!

There was a divine reason why Waverly and I did different things well, and I got into "situations" as I tried to learn a new skill set daily. Once our double income had stopped, I downsized my household expenses to match my budget. The first luxury to go was our weekly pool maintenance service. I carefully watched what the pool technician did on the last day he serviced our pool. This didn't seem like a hard task at all. Nothing I couldn't handle!

The first time I fell into the pool was the first time I brushed down its walls. When the brush reached the bottom, I was supposed to push the algae towards the drain at the deep end of the pool. I missed the lesson on brushing almost parallel to where I was standing on the lanai, and instead brushed towards the center of the pool. My body looked like a professional skier, just before she leaped from the cliff, at a forty-five degree angle to her skis.

I knew for certain that I didn't have the momentum to propel myself back upright, nor did I have the agility to drop the long handle and jump backwards with enough force to keep me standing on the lanai. No, like the Roadrunner and Coyote cartoon, I looked around with a silly grin, checked my pocket for anything that shouldn't get wet, and fell forward into the pool.

When I climbed out, after diving for the long brush handle that had sunk to the bottom at the deep end, I remembered that all of the towels were neatly stacked in a closet inside the house.

Too wet to go inside, and too busy to wait until I dried naturally from the sun, I took all my clothes off and entered the house like a child playing hop scotch across my wood floor – all the way to the closet with the towels. After that day, I made sure that both my feet were squarely on the lanai, no matter how I brushed the walls and bottom of the pool. Lesson learned.

So, the *second* time I went into the pool was the day I was rushing, but had to brush down the *&@! pool first! I noticed that the little bouncing thing holding the chlorine tablets was at one end. I thought I gently pushed it towards the center, but I must have had too much force because it tipped over, and all three chlorine tablets fell into the pool. I had no time for a bathing suit, so I stripped down to my underwear and went into the pool to retrieve the tablets.

Using the long handle and the brush, I inched each of three chlorine tablets up the wall until I could grab them and put them back into the floating container. I expected the tablets to burn my hands if I didn't wear gloves, and the gloves were far, far away. Yes, my palms became irritated. My hair got wet, too, which really disturbed me because now I would be very late for an appointment, looking like a wet pet.

As I exited the pool, soaking wet, I peered into the house at the closet containing the beach towels. Once again, I took everything off, now frustrated and crying about the foolishness of the last half hour. I whimpered out loud as I hop scotched my way to the towels, *"I (sniff) liked Waverly's (deep breath) world better, when we just WROTE CHECKS for every service (sigh)!!"* I then broke into a full cry, which lasted until I was completely dried, dressed, and driving to my destination with a damp head and a bad hairstyle.

For the next few months, I emptied the filter basket, brushed the pool, checked the chemicals in the water, and slapped myself on the back for creating the clear, blue water that greeted me every morning. Then one day, the motor stopped working and the pool was cloudy. Within hours it was a light green, muddy color.

I called the folks who had previously serviced our pool, and they were happy to return to my home. *"When was the last time you backwashed the pool?"* "What's a backwash? I've lived here nearly a decade and never washed the pool, so maybe your guys did it as part of our service plan."

We had installed pools at two of our last three homes, and Waverly maintained them all, including taking apart the filters and probably backwashing as needed. Each time he worked on the pools, I made lunch or went shopping. It never occurred to me that I would outlive him, and be responsible for maintaining our pool! We had spoiled ourselves with a pool service for this house, until Waverly died.

Now I was the "pool person," along with being the "lady of the house" and the "housekeeper." I longed for the return of "Waverly's World" and "Waverly's wealth." While recounting to a friend my dives into the pool wearing my clothes and not a bathing suit, I drew an analogy between my circumstances and Marie Antoinette's.

*"Everything is relative, you know. I mean, in Marie's world, if folks didn't have bread, there was always cake. Hence her naïve, now infamous statement, 'Let them eat cake.' She didn't need to lose her head just because she missed a cue about how the peasants lived. For the past thirty-five years, I was used to writing checks for everything I wanted. When I lacked money in the checking account, I simply used a credit card (my cake). I still have **my** head sitting on my shoulders. Just sayin'!!"*

I don't swim in my pool as often as I did before Waverly died. I was the person who taught him to swim, and he became proficient enough to chase me around the deep end of the pool, pretending he was a shark! I miss seeing him splashing around in the water while I prepared any of our three square meals daily.

It's very lonely swimming by myself, even when I have the joyous sounds of music playing on the intercom system. Yes' that's the same system that awakened me in the middle of the night to loud Rap music! It can be soothing, too.

I don't like sitting at the table on the lanai alone either, staring at the pool and eating a sandwich or drinking a soda without company. But I love when the house is full of noise and laughter, and there is much splashing and eating and drinking. Waverly and I entertained often, so rather than dwell on my normally quiet circumstance, I've kept a pretty lively social schedule that includes enjoying the pool.

Now, I weekly brush down the walls of the pool correctly, check the filter and empty it, check the number of chlorine tablets in the little floating thing, and vacuum the pool bottom monthly. I let the experts at the local pool store tell me what chemicals I need to add, in order to achieve the perfect chemical balance and that gorgeous light blue color. When I get a report that says, "Everything's perfect," I smile to myself, and say, "My compliments to the "pool person!"

Chapter Five
HIS Car!
"You in danger, girl!"

We had two cars, and I knew everything I needed to operate mine while driving no more than fifteen miles over any speed limit. Whenever lights came on, I simply said, *"Oh, Honey, there's a strange light on in my car."* The next time I drove, the light was gone – pure magic!

When he died, I didn't need two cars, so after much pleading, I was able to return my car and keep his. Waverly drove an Audi Q7 with dozens of "bells and whistles," and he mastered all of the technology associated with operating and maintaining the vehicle.

As "first mate," my job was to occasionally rub the driver's neck on long journeys, pass him food and drink, and change the radio station. Never did I assign myself the task of learning how to work the GPS, change settings, open and close the sun roof, check the tire pressure and fuel levels, and very importantly, locate the battery, which turned out to be under the driver's seat instead of under the front hood.

I had seen him twist knobs, press buttons and toggle to input destinations or install CDs. Rather than paying attention, I preferred to check my makeup in the vanity mirror or look out the window at nature.

My first experience with HIS car was figuring out how to change the music in the CD player before I grew to hate the three CDs that were in there two months after he was gone. I kept putting it off, until I decided to read just that portion of the 200-page Audi car manual.

The whole thing was easier than I thought, and I found out that we had the capacity to hold *six* CDs. With the push of an "eject" button and another push on the "load" bar, the old CDs came out easily. With a couple of gentle pushes in reverse, the new CDs were in place, and I had my choice of six kinds of music daily, plus the radio and Sirius Satellite stations. I was a technology genius who had access to news and tunes, all with the push of a few carefully chosen buttons!

Tackling the GPS System was a radically different situation! The manual devoted a dozen pages to it, so I vowed never to use it. I reasoned that I'd be just fine stopping at gas stations and asking for directions if I got lost. The computerized map on the large screen right in front of me was of no interest to me, despite the fact that I did know that the little blue arrow showed the driver going from Point A to Point B.

You'll remember that my precious husband was an organ donor. I was pleasantly surprised when The Organ and Tissue Donation Institute folks called within two weeks of the Home Going Celebration to see how I was doing. My first thought was that they were just checking on the status of my organs and tissues, which they would claim upon my death. Instead, I found a group of nurturing, compassionate people who considered their jobs more privilege than work.

During their third call a few months later, I mentioned that I was keeping a journal to heal my mind and spirit. They said I was doing better than most recent widows, and felt that perhaps I could be a comfort to those having a more difficult time than I. They invited me to a meeting dedicated to those who recently lost loved ones.

Despite their confidence in my inner strength, I hoped to gain a strategy for dealing with the sadness that came over me without warning, sometimes lasting moments and sometimes hours. I felt I had been crying too often, and I wanted some relief that I prayed would come from a gathering of people experiencing the same confusion, depression and loneliness as I.

I left the house in plenty of time to get to the meeting, half an hour away. When I realized that I was lost and late, I silently chastised myself for never learning the navigation system, which would have delivered driver and vehicle to the front steps of the destination on time. I pulled into a small parking lot, determined to find in the 200-page manual the section on navigating the GPS. When I found it, the words didn't seem like they were written in English, but the accompanying pictures helped me greatly.

Within five minutes, I had toggled my way to identifying the city, street and street number of The Organ and Tissue Donation Institute. The familiar pleasant voice in the car announced, *"Your route is being calculated."* Within a second, the voice directed me to make a left turn from the parking lot onto the street in front of me. Proud of myself, I did as directed, and waited for the next turn. I was grinning now!

Nine seconds later, the voice said, *"You have reached your destination."* As I looked up to see the building I had been looking for, I murmured loudly to myself, *"That ain't even right. Not fair at all!"* I pulled into the parking lot, locked the car, and gave it a cold stare as I headed for the building.

Alas, I had mastered the navigation system that day, and by the time I found the group of grieving persons to which I belonged, everyone was crying as one widow was sharing her personal story. Without hearing the beginning of her story, I cried, too. I wondered if I were in the right place to learn to shed tears *less* often, which was my primary objective. The second one was, of course, conquering GPS, and clearly I had met that objective!

On another occasion, I recalled that my car showed a yellow light that looked like an exclamation point surrounded by parentheses. I remembered that this symbol indicated that we needed air in one or more tires, or that we had a flat tire.

If it were a flat tire, Waverly retrieved the spare that was recessed behind the six passenger seats. He changed the tire, got the old one fixed, and returned the spare to its fitted space. If it were a tire pressure issue, Waverly took the air gauge, determined the amount of air needed to meet the requirement in each tire, drove to a gas station and solved the problem while I waited in the passenger seat, reading a book or thinking of nothing in particular.

On this day, I ignored the problem for one hour after seeing the little icon, so words appeared in the panel where the symbol had been, telling me, *"Check your tire pressure."* I understood the *first* warning, but was busy at the moment.

It seemed almost immediately that the yellow light turned orange, and the words disappeared. All I could think of was Whoppi Goldberg's line in GHOST, *"You in danger, girl!"* I supposed that if the color had to turn red to "drive" me to action, the car would have a real attitude and refuse to enter the next busy intersection.

Too embarrassed to go to a gas station without at least knowing how many pounds of pressure were supposed to be in each tire, I went home to study the manual and have a stiff drink. After reading a dozen pages devoted to wheels and tires, I found a chart that had different information for a "normal" and a "full load" of passengers (There's a difference?). At the end of the chart, it said, *"This information can also be found on the inside panel of the driver's door."* I shouted obscenities at the manual and its author for making that the last, and not the first sentence! I'd take care of the problem tomorrow.

Later that night, when I opened my Facebook page, a strange woman posted that she saw my profile and thought I was "hot." She offered to "web chat" with me. Obviously, there were TWO things she didn't know about me!! I decided at *that* moment that it had been a long, frustrating day, and it was time to go to bed. I took great comfort in the fact that I knew where my bed was and how to get in it!

The next morning, my pastor helped me figure out where to stick the tire gauge that Waverly kept in the car. I'm now a professional "requester of help," since I couldn't even screw the tiny caps on the tires straight. My nails were too long, and besides, I might have chipped the polish. I did feel the difference in the ride when all my tires were properly inflated, though, and the blank screen in front of my steering wheel affirmed that the car computer was satisfied with my performance.

That morning was also cold, that is, cold for Florida at forty-nine degrees. I took pride in stumbling on a button that heated my whole seat. However, I must have hit "steam," because my bottom and back were cooking as I tried in vain to remember the button I had pushed while trying to turn the radio on.

The good news was that the music sounded great! Nevertheless, I envisioned smoke coming from the rear of my clothing as I exited the car. I felt warm all over! Good thing for me it was cold outside.

Then there was that time when I had an appointment to take the Audi for service. Since I discovered that the car could talk to me, I ascribed sentences never actually uttered, that I knew the car was *thinking*. As soon as I set the GPS for the dealership some distance away, I thought I heard, *"Thank God an intelligent life form is going to tune me up today. All my fluids are depleted."*

While I was admiring those sparkling wheel covers and perfectly inflated tires, the service manager came out to say that it was time for me to purchase four new tires. Since these had taken me 44,000 miles without incident, it was prudent to get the same model and size, which, including the charge for alignment would cost only $2,000.00! Was he kidding? "Didn't we used to buy whole cars for that price?" He chuckled and returned to the shop. I kicked the tire nearest me before driving home to ponder my next move.

My pastor, who helped me inflate the tires that now needed replacing, pointed me in the direction of a tire company that would give me duplicate tires for far less than the dealership. "Waverly always took our cars straight to the dealership for everything, and I don't know if he'd approve of me doing otherwise." *"Trust me* (I said he was a pastor). *You'll be pleased, and Waverly would applaud you for saving money, big time!"* He was right and I was happy. I dared the car to honk its horn in protest!!

Recently, the panel in front of me that gives me symbols and expressions displayed the words, *"Service Due."* The premier service contract with the dealership had expired, and to my surprise, I found that the tire company also serviced vehicles. Wow! Only in America, right?

Two days had elapsed before I made the appointment for service. During that time, the panel in front of me got my attention while I was driving, with these words: *"Service Now."* Within half an hour, the words on the display panel included an exclamation mark: *"Service Due! Now!"*

Really? Seriously? My car dared to add not one, but *two* exclamation marks to show disgust with me? No doubt it "heard" that I was a former high school English teacher who would immediately understand the nuance *that* punctuation brought to a command sentence.

I got the message, and *told* the car I was considering trading it in for a horse and a bucket of feed. I wouldn't have to deal with insults or the high price of premium gas any longer. The car was serviced, and the sentence about needing service, including that exclamation mark, disappeared from my view.

With hands tightly gripped around the steering wheel, I wondered what the next altercation between HIS car and me would be. I didn't have to wait long before I again hit that heated seat function while trying to change the radio station and keep my eyes on the road.

Last time that happened, the memory eventually cancelled the unwanted warming service, and my rear no longer smoked when I exited the vehicle. Today it was ninety-six degrees in Central Florida! So while cool air blew on my face and arms, scorching heat cooked my back and butt.

I suffered all the way home, then read the section in that thick manual that addressed heated seats. Now, who thought it was a good idea to place that button right next to the one for the radio? Wouldn't it have made more sense to add this function to the side of the seat, enabling me to adjust it to eight positions and *choose* to add heat? I know I'm right!

Yesterday, while leaving my driveway, and fidgeting aimlessly with the toggle mechanism (Why, oh, Why?), I involuntarily lurched forward, narrowly avoiding mowing down the mailbox of my neighbor across the street. Phew! My brakes saved it. Had I just discovered the cruise control? That's a perfectly useful tool to have at my disposal while driving in and out of my cul-de-sac!

Then, there was the time I was driving in traffic, and someone stopped without warning ahead of me. As I hit my brakes, I must have inadvertently moved the gear with my right hand into the "Sport" position. I know this because all of a sudden, my car sounded like I was at the Daytona Speedway, racing around a track. It was a loud sound, like an engine roaring. I looked to my left and right, disgusted that some driver was showing off in heavy traffic.

That is, I thought it was someone else's car, until I noticed that the sound followed ME as I accelerated and slowed to a stop after that quick step on my brakes. It was I who made all that noise, and if I remembered correctly from the times where Waverly deliberately used the Sport gear, it was I who had begun to waste gas!

Waverly used the Sport feature when we were on long trips, and another driver on the road late at night dared to pass us. He took it as a personal affront, and "dropped into Sport gear," after which we moved in lightening speed and overtook the audacious driver of the other car. It was a matter of respect, after all! Shortly after we won each racing challenge, we stopped to refuel!

To date, I've read and internalized thirty-nine pages of the two-hundred-page Audi Q7 manual, and I'm super proud of myself. There's no need to read further until the talking car tells me to do something unfamiliar!

Waverly used to have the car washed weekly, purchasing the top package. He had it detailed quarterly. My new widow's austerity budget didn't include such luxury, so I have managed to get the top package car wash offered at the local gas station, bi-weekly! As for detailing, it will have to be someone's Christmas gift to MY Audi and me. I'm sure if the car could speak, it would ask, *"Where's my Daddy? Mommy's mean and ignorant, and my white exterior is too often dusty-looking!"* No response needed from me because I agree!

Chapter Six
Mama Said There'd Be Days Like This!

"Weeping may endure for a night, but joy cometh in the morning."
Psalm 30:5

The first critically sad moment for me came during the first summer without Waverly. We had made plans to go to the New Jersey Shore in June, as we had done for over twenty years. I discussed with my family whether or not I should go, and the consensus was that I try to follow as normal a schedule as possible. My brother said, *"Waverly would not want you to stay home and miss the beauty and relaxation of the Atlantic Ocean. You need to get away anyway, and you've already booked the vacation."*

Two dear friends and my brother-in-law planned to come to my resort, each staying at least a day and night. There would be some private time in between visitors, but I thought I would enjoy some quiet, reflective time during the week at the New Jersey Shore. I decided to go.

This was the first time I flew there, since Waverly and I always drove the seventeen hours, stopping only for food and gas. I took the airport shuttle to the resort, quickly realizing that I had no transportation unless I hailed a cab. I decided to walk to the store for some groceries to entertain my friends and relatives when they arrived.

I was careful not to load the shopping cart with too much, since I would be walking over a mile back to the resort while carrying groceries. I ended up with three full bags, which proved to be heavier than I predicted. I walked and stopped, rested the bags on the sidewalk, then walked and stopped again. No taxi came my way, and I would never hitchhike, even if someone were willing to stop.

I heard the sound of someone walking fast behind me, and I moved over to let the person pass. A woman scooped up the heaviest of my bags, both asking and insisting that she carry it to my destination. Turned out she was staying at the same resort, and I was convinced that God had sent this Angel to assist me with the groceries.

While unpacking my suitcase, I cried because I always put Waverly's clothes in the top two drawers and mine in the bottom two. I stared at the empty top two drawers of the dresser before putting my things in the bottom two drawers. And putting only my toiletries in the

25

bathroom caused a new wave of tears. I literally told myself to dry it up because folks were giving up their time to be with me, and they wouldn't know how to console me if I cried during their whole visit.

My first set of company came and went, and we all cried a little, missing Waverly. I brought the scrapbook I had prepared after breaking down the funeral collage. There were pictures, cards and tributes providing an assemblage of fond memories. We all shed a few tears looking at the scrapbook. Nevertheless, we ate and drank, swam in the ocean and had fun. I slept well the night my brother-in-law's family stayed overnight. Then they left.

There was one full day before my next company arrived, and I looked forward to walking on the beach right outside my suite. I packed some drinks and fruit, snacks and suntan oil, a blanket and a towel. The moment I stepped onto the sand of the beach, I became sullen. I was overcome with sadness because, as I scanned all the people enjoying the day, it appeared to me that *everyone* was with *someone* and *only I* was alone. It was a horrible feeling that took my breath away.

I sensed that every person stopped having fun to stare at me. I backed up onto the steps leading back to the resort, and ran fast to my suite. I dropped my things on the floor, and sank to the floor next to them. I don't remember crying that hard since the initial shock of Waverly's death.

How would I survive until the second set of company arrived? I couldn't go back to the beach to be gawked at by strangers. Why did I come in the first place? Was everyone except *me* a couple or a family? I had brought the *HOLY BIBLE* with me, but before I opened it, I lay on the couch with a glass of wine in my hand, and closed my eyes in meditation.

I remembered the first time I met Waverly's family. His parents were Deacons in their church, and they raised their four boys in a Christian home. Every Sunday, the blessing before dinner consisted of each person at the table reciting from memory his or her favorite Biblical verse. Pop Baskerville wouldn't allow anyone to get away with saying, *"Jesus wept."* The quote had to be substantive, which to Pop meant lengthy. Without this ritual recitation, there would be no dinner for the heathen at the table.

Waverly's favorite passage was this one: **Psalm 121:1-2:** *"I will lift up mine eyes to the hills, from whence cometh my help; My help cometh from the Lord, which made heaven and earth."* For my first Sunday dinner with Waverly's family, I, too, had learned to recite a verse: **Proverbs 3:5-6:** *"Trust in the Lord with all thine heart; and lean not unto thine own understanding. In all thy* *ways, acknowledge him, and he shall direct thy paths."*

Wow, I hadn't thought about those passages in a long time, since we abandoned the Baskerville family practice in our home on Sundays. We did, however, bless the food before every meal, whether we were home or out in public.

That happy memory caused me to feel better. Those scriptures reminded me that I could get through my first vacation without Waverly, and have fun like I always had at the beach. I just needed to stop feeling sorry for myself.

Besides, it was time for me to recognize the special efforts my family members and friends were making to visit me during that week. Where was my gratitude? I regained my composure and my pleasant disposition. I knew in my heart that no one on the beach paid attention to me. No one gawked, snickered, or belittled me for being a single person on a beach at the Atlantic Ocean. It was all in my mind, where my "pity party" had just started. That party abruptly ended!

I didn't go back to the beach without having people around me, but I ceased being paranoid about what beachgoers were thinking. I actually had a good time after that.

I brought my journal on the trip, in which I wrote down my feelings daily. The entries for that week went from feeling lonely and isolated to being grateful for family and friends who surrounded me with tenderness and patience. They fed me and entertained me, and loved me sincerely. Who could ask for anything more? I returned to Florida, glad I had gone to the Jersey Shore after all!

The day before what would have been my forty-fifth wedding anniversary was the second most tear-filled day since Waverly died. I woke up that morning, kneeling for my usual prayer thanking God for another day, and promising to be productive and patient. But before I could utter a word, I started sobbing and shouting, "So what's next? What happens now? What is it that you want me to do alone that I couldn't do with Waverly, God What do you want of me? WHAT?!!"

I know we're not supposed to talk to God like that, but the "one day-one blessing at a time" thing wasn't working for me. Wasn't I able to fulfill my divine purpose in life while standing next to Waverly? I went from my parents' home to my husband's home, so God must have known that I wasn't meant to be alone! What was He thinking?

I didn't thank Him for my daily abundance of blessings, and I didn't pray for anyone else that day. I must have shown the minimum respect by saying "Amen," but cried getting dressed and walking Lucky. I cried because I couldn't find the Staples coupon for the ink cartridge

I needed, and then because I couldn't find one sneaker. I made it a point to keep busy with a number of tasks, but wiped away the steady stream of tears while doing them all. I got angry with myself because I made my eyes puffy, and then I cried about that.

I involuntarily knelt down by the living room coffee table sometime before dinner, loudly asking God questions in rapid succession. "Did you take Waverly because his work was done, or because you had something for me to do that I would never see until he was gone from me? Couldn't you have given me a sign, despite the HOLY BIBLE saying 'we know not the hour of our death,' or something like that? I wasn't ready! If You never make mistakes, God, then help me to make sense of this. I need Waverly, I want to hold him and kiss him – just one more time, OK? I want to say goodbye to my 'Darling Forever' until we meet again."

I just didn't understand what was happening to me, and I could find no solace. I was sobbing uncontrollably now, full of despair. At that moment, my daughter, Alicia called. Her family was almost home from spending Thanksgiving in Atlanta with her in-laws, but she sensed that I needed her. I knew it was futile to hide my state of mind, so I continued crying. I was actually hoarse from so much weeping.

She and Bruce and the four grandchildren drove straight to my house to see about me. Their presence always lifted my spirits, and this evening was no exception. They had driven eight hours, and needed to get home and rest. Yet they came to comfort me. So I pulled myself together to assure them that I'd be fine when they left.

By late evening when I was home alone again, I felt terrible about the way I had behaved all day. God could have sent me a stern message, borrowing a line in the movie, *Taxi Driver*: *"You talkin' ta ME?"* I owed Him a more gracious prayer that night, and I knew I had better pray for someone besides my sorry self! Tomorrow would be better.

I knelt down and bowed my head, thanking God especially for this day that tested my faith, understanding and patience. I thanked Him for the profusion of love from my family and friends, and for allowing me almost forty-five years with my true love. I thanked God for taking Waverly so quickly and painlessly, without his lingering or experiencing discomfort or losing his dignity. We can't choose our exit from this life, but if we could, we'd opt for a quick and painless transition like my Waverly encountered.

I promised to *try* to follow His spiritual path by faith, since I couldn't see the plan right then. Patience was never my strength, and I confessed to God that the night Waverly came home from the hospital and couldn't rest, I was irritable because I, too, couldn't rest. Had I made him feel inadequate because he couldn't help interrupting my sleep? While saying out loud that I regretted losing patience with my sick husband, I began wailing again!

A soft voice inside of me caused me to make another promise to God: "Since I can't change anything I did or said before Waverly died, I WILL go forward consciously TRYING to exercise daily patience with everyone around me." I drew comfort from the thought of replacing that guilt with a commitment to change something unflattering about myself. Before rising from my praying position, I asked God to help me keep my patience pledge. *"Amen. Amen."*

I slept deeply that night, possibly from crying so hard so long, but also because I believed God closed my eyes to ensure my undisturbed rest. When I awoke the next morning, I remembered the Biblical passage *"Weeping may endure for a night, but joy cometh in the morning."* (**Psalm 30:5**). I had regained my normally positive, strong state of mind, and I was ready to help someone else in order to help myself.

God *had*, in fact, answered my questions by giving me the title of another chapter in this book: *"Mama Said There'd Be Days Like This!"* I heard the title of that old song as clearly as if God had sat across from me and spoke the seven words. Yes, I now understood that I needed a chapter to express those emotions and incidences that were plainly miserable. The epiphany for me was to realize that humor and grief were inseparable, appearing both purposefully and randomly in my life in tandem.

Waverly loved the holidays, and we always had amazing decorations and hosted most of the family gatherings. I was glad I opted to decorate and to host Christmas Day, instead of turning my first Christmas without my mate into a "private pity party." By the time the grandchildren left, my home was *fully* decorated and I was humming Christmas carols! While checking emails, I noticed that there were no tears on the keyboard of my computer. I was definitely making progress.

Later that evening, Alicia called because she was remembering the last time she saw her Daddy. It was in the hospital the week before he died, and she had just kissed him goodbye for the evening. As she left the room, she instinctively turned to glance at him, and he was sitting in the chair near the bed, staring out the window at the rain. *"He looked so sad and I wanted to run back and kiss him again, but then I thought maybe he wanted to be alone with his thoughts."*

My heart ached when I thought my Waverly might have felt isolated, maybe afraid and too proud to show vulnerability to his grown child. I shared with her that twice in the hospital, her Dad awoke in the middle of the night in a panic. "He pulled the wires connected to the monitors from his chest and arms and got out of bed, searching for me. He said he could hear me speaking nearby, but couldn't find me."

Tears poured down my face and rested on my neck, as I said, "Oh, God! I wonder if that was a foreshadowing of his death because as soon as the paramedics arrived, someone ushered me away from Daddy to ask me questions. He kept my face turned away from what they were doing, but maybe Daddy was searching for me in his mind because he could hear me talking. If he couldn't speak, but knew I was at his side, I should have held his hand."

"No, Mommy, you would have been in the way. You had vital information to share. You also called ME, and I told the kids we had to hurry to help Grandpa. You couldn't have done anything differently." Intellectually, I knew she was right, but psychologically, I was filled with doubt, pain and second-guessing something I couldn't change.

Should I have done anything differently during Waverly's last moments? My daughter and I cried together before ending our phone conversation. This moment brought us even closer. We were both physically and emotionally exhausted and needed to get to sleep.

In mid-January, I was driving home from a meeting, and I had gotten to the point in my grieving where I no longer cried at the thought of coming home to an empty house (except for Lucky), which was a good thing. But for some reason, I almost burst into tears while driving, because half an hour's distance from my home, my mind recollected the last two days I was with Waverly.

As soon as he got home from the hospital that Sunday evening in March, the phone rang constantly with happy fans wanting to speak to him. He seemed uneasy, and when we had a calm moment together, he said, *"I don't want people to think I'm OK, just because I'm out of the hospital. I'm not well yet."* My response was, "You're right, Honey. I'm so glad you're home, but I'll be sure everyone knows that you're still sick and we will be finding out what's wrong soon. Don't worry. I'll handle the callers." Still, I know he felt encouraged knowing how many people were praying and pulling for his recovery.

After a light dinner, we were both tired and went to bed. He climbed the stairs independently, but his walk was slow, and he sat in a chair as soon as he reached the bedroom. I tried not to notice, turning on the television and getting him some cold water. He seemed better, and climbed into bed with little assistance.

Waverly woke up three times to use the bathroom, and I had to lead him there each time and wait to usher him back to bed. That's where I exhibited the impatience I later confessed to God through deeply remorseful tears.

The next night, which turned out to be our last together, Waverly offered to sleep in the guest bedroom so he wouldn't disturb me. No way! We took our usual sleeping positions, with our legs wrapped around each other and Waverly gently stroking my back as we both fell asleep. I felt like all was right with the world again, since we were committed to doing whatever it took for his full recovery.

When we awoke, I praised him for sleeping through the night. His response was, *"I made myself stay in bed all night without getting up."* I pondered the difficulty of the task he left undefined, as I asked what he wanted for breakfast, and went downstairs to prepare it and bring it to him. When I returned with a mushroom omelet, toast and tea, he was standing at the door to the balcony, having already put on his shirt and underwear. *"It's nice outside. Let's eat outside this morning, OK?"* It was absolutely OK with me.

Waverly didn't eat the bread and didn't finish the omelet, which worried, but didn't alarm me. I took the dishes downstairs, and when I returned, ready to escort him to the bedroom to dress for the doctors' visits, he was in the bedroom putting on his sweat pants. He was always fiercely independent, and I respected that. He wanted a different pair of shoes from the ones I chose, so I made the switch and tied his shoelaces.

He asked me to go downstairs ahead of him and he would follow. I obeyed. When he descended the stairs and walked into the kitchen without assistance, I was making our lunch to eat between the two appointments. Waverly sat at his usual seat at the table, clipping his fingernails and saying he wanted me to make an appointment for him to get a manicure and pedicure when he felt better. He left a small pile of nail clippings on the table, which I would clean up later.

When it was time to go, he did let me lead him to the car, asking for help getting his legs in position to close the passenger door. We had a pleasant conversation about the news on the radio, our schedule for the day, and our plans for the evening when we finished with the doctors.

We got to the parking lot of the doctor's office and he got out of the car without my help, but leaned against a parked car until I parked ours and could walk in front of him while he held onto my shoulders with his hands. We completed the paperwork, and I commented, "Wow, Honey, look at all the check marks of symptoms you have." He gave me a slight grin, and we both sat silently until the doctor's receptionist called us into his office.

At that time, it seemed normal that he nodded off while I read a book. He wasn't sleeping well nights, so often he napped during the day while sitting in a comfortable chair. I decided not to wake him until we had to get up and meet the doctor.

While I kept driving and crying, I wondered if, during those quiet moments before he collapsed and died, he were thinking about God or me or dying. Did he know how sick he was and not tell me? Was he surprised like me?

Was he afraid of dying because his physical movement was slow and he didn't know the cause? Had he clipped his fingernails at the kitchen table in preparation to meet his Maker, or done it because he was self-conscious about his appearance? Had he been daily pushing through the fear and anxiousness about his condition, only to give up for the split-second of weakness that was fatal?

I had been deep in thought about all of this, when I recognized my street in front of me. My car must have automatically driven half an hour until it brought me to my destination. I certainly didn't remember driving through each traffic light until I turned into my cul-de-sac. Even though I knew I would be in my driveway within a minute, I couldn't help returning to my deep thoughts about Waverly's last day with me.

I had a hard time thinking of him going through silent pain or being fearful and not sharing his thoughts with me. And yet, it would have been his preference to save me from joining him in worrying about what the doctors would find. I chose to believe that, like me, Waverly was eager to follow our schedule that day of seeing two doctors, after which we hoped to get a diagnosis and an action plan we would faithfully follow.

I couldn't stop weeping as I exited and locked my car in the driveway. I cried as I turned the key into the front door, entering the empty home, except for the happy sound of Lucky welcoming me. I was sobbing, catching my breath between cries, and nothing could assuage my pain.

I didn't know what was happening to me, because I initially had happy thoughts while driving home. I didn't know why I couldn't gain my composure as quickly as I normally did. I was momentarily lost, despondent.

I wasn't ready for this quite sudden change in my mood, without warning. Even when I brushed my teeth before going to bed, I was weeping. When I lay down, enough tears fell on my pillow to wet the pillowcase. I was sad, lonely, insecure and afraid of tomorrow. I likened the grief process to having a merciless opponent in battle. Each time I let down my guard, "Grief" punched me hard in my weakest spot. I was never able to brace for the hit. Unhappy doubts, feelings of guilt and regret came and went like the ebb and flow of the ocean – never-ending.

I asked God to help my mind stop racing so I could rest. I had a pounding headache by then, and needed sleep. He must have obliged, because as soon as my head touched the pillow, I slept soundly until morning. When I awoke, I was calm and reflective about that last day with my husband. My headache didn't leave, though, until I had my morning coffee and two aspirin.

As I drank, I pondered my quandary. Waverly and I had gone to the doctor's office together that last morning of his life, but an hour later, I was leaving the hospital without him. I'd never see him again in this life! I recognized that I had to develop his kind of discernment and independence, but I was unsure of how or where to begin learning that. My "life skills teacher" was gone, and I hadn't paid full attention to my lessons. What ever would I do now?

I opened the *HOLY BIBLE* for solace, and randomly turned to **Isaiah 25-26**. The third verse of Chapter 26 said, *"Thou wilt keep Him in perfect peace, whose mind is stayed on Thee; because he trusteth in thee."* I read the whole chapter, but that verse especially eased my mind.

Around that time, Alicia explained that she put bereavement tears into three categories. *"You might wipe them with two fingertips, or two knuckles, or two palms. That represents three increasing levels of the flow and intensity of shedding tears! I try to stop at 'finger-finger,' but sometimes I'm at 'palm-palm' and I just grab a bigger box of tissues."* I had never categorized the depth of my tears, but this was insightful.

I awoke one morning to calculate that my father was born one hundred-fifteen years ago. He was a generation older than my Mom, whose birthday was two days after his. He died at age seventy and she at age seventy-six. I had been thinking about my parents for a couple of days, as I wrestled with the sorrow that each April brought. Both their birthdays were in April. The weather had been overcast and chilly this particular morning, which didn't help change my mood from gloomy to sunny.

I missed my parents terribly, but I had never experienced the ache that permeated my body when I lost my Darling Forever. It's not that I loved my parents less, but the love between children and parents is different from the love of mates who shared an intimacy for nearly half a century.

I couldn't rationally explain how my mind jumped from missing my parents to again longing for Waverly. Maybe I just needed my morning coffee and a walk with Lucky to bring clarity to my head – once again.

While drinking that strong coffee as I walked her, I looked up at the magnificent sky. I barely noticed the sky while I was working for forty-two years. There was always a destination, a meeting or event, and a limited time to get there. Since my retirement, and more so since becoming a widow, I look at the sky daily in wonderment. God had always treated me to a tapestry of intricate cloud patterns and blended colors that I was only now appreciating.

Typical of Florida, it started to rain hard without warning. I couldn't have a bad day AND a bad hair day! I deliberately changed my attitude as I took my wet self and my wet dog inside.

Before checking emails, I sometimes went to Waverly's funeral website, where folks posted messages to him and me for a year. I felt confident enough to go there without reaching for tissues, but "palm-palm" level tears overtook me when I read the first message.

There was a post from my daughter, Alicia. Her middle name is the same as mine -- LaVerne, and though she spent her young years asking what she had done in my womb to deserve that name, she affectionately used "Vern-Vern" on occasion, only with her father.

This was her post:

"I can't seem to get the word surreal out of my mind! This whole experience has seemed like such an odd dream from which I have been looking extremely forward to waking, yet it never seems to end. Funny, I always thought an unending dream would be something happier and lighter, but this is quite the opposite. My heart aches for a number of reasons and for a number of people, but mostly for my dear Mommy.

I am reminded of that precious Luther Vandross song, Dance With My Father...

> *'If I could steal one final glance, One final step,*
> *One final dance with him,*
> *I'd play a song that would never ever end,*
> *Cause I'd love, love, love to*
> *Dance with my father again.*

Sometimes I'd listen outside her door,
And I'd hear how Mama would cry for him.
I'd pray for her even more than me,
I'd pray for her even more than me.
I know I'm praying for much too much,
But could you send her
The only man she loved.
I know you don't do it usually,
But Dear Lord She's dying
To dance with my father again."

I love you forever, Daddy. Vern-Vern

Reading that post made me stop working altogether. I stared at the computer screen, almost screaming because I realized how deeply hurt my daughter was, and still she prayed for God to ease *my* pain. *"Surreal"* was an apt expression to sum up our dreamlike state of mind. But every daily awakening produced the same emptiness because her Daddy, my Darling was gone. I had become crestfallen again in an instant, with no warning.

I couldn't get the song out of my head, as I tormented myself remembering the last time Waverly drew me close to him with a firm embrace. I was always safe in his arms, no matter the danger before us. Frantically, I looked through the loose photos that hadn't yet been placed in an album, trying to find the last one we took together. I needed to see it and touch it immediately!

It turned out to be a picture of a happy occasion at our home with the grandchildren surrounding Waverly and me. I framed it and displayed it. The completed task brought me less consolation than I expected, but I wasn't sorry for the effort.

Then I stared repeatedly at that picture, suddenly gripped by the realization that I'd never again experience the physical and emotional intimacy that I enjoyed for so many years. I told myself that I had been blessed with more happiness than most persons I knew, but the tears flowed faster. Alicia didn't offer a category for tears flowing harder and faster than "palm-palm" could handle.

In the absence of a tissue box nearby, I used "sleeve-sleeve" to wipe away these tears. It was no use because I couldn't be consoled, not even by my sensible mind. I didn't call anyone to help me process this. It was just too personal and painful.

The weight of that realization buckled my spirit. The rest of my life would be void of daily companionship, of being caressed each night as I fell asleep, of making love, of waking next to someone who instinctively offered a corrective action for every disagreeable situation into which I brought us. Despondent, I didn't think I could bear that future. So then, why was I beginning each day thanking God for more life? I was overcome with depression and despair and fear, in equal portions.

My going through previously sad or unpleasant circumstances over the years had never caused me to shut out the sunlight and crawl under the bed covers without connecting with someone who loved me. For the first time, the thought of taking that negative, dangerous step of giving in to despair pervaded my being. I couldn't shake it.

I turned to the *HOLY BIBLE*, thrusting it open in hopes of receiving a message from God. I did! It was **Psalm 23** – *"The Lord is my shepherd, I shall not want....."* I had memorized that passage as a child, but this time, each word jumped off the page, as if to almost literally soothe me. I wiped my face and kept reading. I began to feel hopeful about my recovery from mourning and grief because *"Thou art with me."*

Shortly after that, my pastor and his wife came over for dinner and a movie. They brought, *Return to Me*, starring Minnie Driver. It wasn't a new movie, but I hadn't seen it. We made popcorn and set our snacks and drinks on snack trays in front of the television.

The first scene was of Minnie, playing a character about to die unless she received a heart transplant. Then we saw the happy life of a couple that got into a terrible car accident. The wife died, and soon the audience became aware that our main character received that wife's healthy heart. This reaffirmed my faith in the importance of organ donation. So far, so good!

The "plot thickened," until all was revealed towards the end of the movie. I wiped a tear when the wife died, because I could relate to her husband feeling despondent without her. Their dog felt the same way. I recalled how my Lucky sat next to Waverly's seat at our kitchen table for months after he died. I followed the rest of the movie without relating any of its contents to my life.

However, at the end, when the husband of the deceased courted our Minnie, he told his friends that while he missed his wife immensely, he *"ached"* for this woman. He *"needed"* to spend the rest of his life with her, and couldn't live without her. He was grateful for a second chance at love.

At that moment, before their final embrace and the rolling credits at the end of the movie, I think I had a meltdown, an inability to control my emotions! I had cried hard in public only a few times, preferring to share my feelings privately with God in the quiet of my home. But just then, I heard myself falling into a hysterical state of mind, as I ran to the kitchen weeping loudly and grabbing a large square of towel paper with which to cover my face.

I leaned over the kitchen sink, unable to catch my breath. I shouted in distress, "I'll never again have that oneness that this couple found. I won't ever have a second chance at love, or ache to be with anyone but Waverly, and that means I'll be alone the rest of my life. I've never been alone before. I don't know if I can bear it."

Hopelessness overtook me, and I didn't care to hide my fragile emotional state from my movie companions. They gently caressed me, but I never stopped crying. I had brought forth from the recesses of my mind a truth I never wanted to speak out loud.

My pastor asked us all to sit at the kitchen table while he offered a prayer for my healing. By the time he finished praying that God relieve my anxiety, I had gained my composure. I was crying softly, now listening to the words meant to comfort me, which they did. My friends apologized for their movie choice, but I assured them that it was a wonderful movie. The problem was with *me*, not the movie.

One calm July morning, Alicia and Bruce were shopping in *Bed, Bath & Beyond*, when Bruce saw a person whose appearance was too close to Waverly's for comfort. He called Alicia to see for herself how tall the man was, the shape of his head and ears, how he wore his suspenders, even his gait and hands in his pockets.

They went to two different aisles, looking to see the face of the man, who was always walking in front of them. When they left the store, using both doors for them and their four children to exit, the man was already outside, once more walking ahead of them. He had no purchases in his hands, which were still in his pockets. They took a picture with their phone camera and sent it to me.

I choked up a little seeing it. I wanted to rush to the individual, spin him around and look into his eyes. I wanted it to BE Waverly, and I longed to be held tightly in his arms while he told me everything would be all right. When the chilling reality gripped me again, my feelings were like jangled discords, with nothing making sense.

I prayed for guidance and comfort, and what came into my head was that angels surround us to ease our pain through spirits and dreams. This may have been a real person, but it may also have been one of those angels, watching over Alicia and her family. The person kept enough distance to observe the family, but remained out of reach every time Alicia and her husband moved about the store, trying to get a glimpse of his face.

Shortly after the incident, I went to San Diego on vacation with my college friends from the State University College at Fredonia in Upstate New York. The four of us, plus Waverly, had been friends for forty-seven years! And we called ourselves the BFFFFs (Best Friends Forever From Fredonia).

The trip to San Diego was planned before Waverly died, and we reserved two villas large enough for the two couples to have bedrooms, and the two single friends to sleep on the pull out sofa in the living room of the larger unit.

Once Waverly passed away, we discussed at length whether any of us should go on the trip. In the end, we cancelled the smaller villa and kept the larger one for *one* couple and three single women. My best friend's husband decided to stay home, so the four females could be together as "girls."

I had an amazing, happy time with them. We laughed constantly, with a disproportionate amount of laughter directed at me! I experienced the sensation of a slumber party for the first time since I was a child. We didn't need to keep up appearances for the men in our lives. Through the laughter and a few tears, I drew enough strength from my BFFFF embraces and conversations to carry me for a good while when I got home.

Still, after all that gaiety, fun and fellowship, I was apprehensive while driving home from the airport. The reason was that, on the car radio came the voice of Luther Vandross singing, *A House is Not a Home*. By the time I heard the words, *"...when I climb the stairs and there's no one there...I'm not meant to live alone...turn this house into a home,"* I was weeping so hard that I gasped for air. It didn't matter that the song was about a couple separated, because for me, it was about separation through death.

I turned the radio off, vowing to stay away from Luther for a little while. I *used* to love his songs! I looked forward to the day where I could listen to Waverly's favorite songs by artists like *The Manhattans* or anything *Motown*, and not break down.

I had reached home around 1:00 a.m. I parked the car, pulled my luggage through the garage into the house, and sat on the floor at the bottom of the staircase to my bedroom. My sweet companion, Lucky was at my sister's house until the next morning, so the house was really empty and quiet. I didn't even unpack or read the pile of mail I had retrieved from the mailbox. I ascended the stairs quickly and knelt down to pray before crying myself to sleep.

The next day, I retrieved some literature that I was given at the hospital where Waverly died. It offered grief counseling to persons who recently lost loved ones. I hadn't thrown it away, so perhaps I saved it because I recognized subconsciously that I would need professional help. I made the call, as my palms began to sweat. The voice was that of the Spiritual Care Chaplain who had met me at the hospital that grim March day months ago.

She remembered me, and my daughter and grandchildren. She said there weren't answers to those nagging "what if" and "why me or mine" questions, so I must focus on the wonderful times my husband and I shared all of our adult lives. She said she was expecting my call, but only when I was emotionally ready to receive professional help. I was ready.

Chapter Seven
Grief Counseling, a "Must"

"The only way to get to the other side is to go through the door."
Helen Keller

It was September when I entered the hospital for the second time since Waverly died five months earlier. I had made it through the "Service of Remembrance" last month, where the Spiritual Care Chaplains prepared a beautiful tribute to all their patients who had died the previous year. That event brought me to uncontrollable tears, so I was apprehensive about my reaction to receiving grief counseling at the same site.

I signed up for a six-week class run by two Chaplains from the Spiritual Care Department of the hospital. It was called "Successfully Managing Grief." As I pulled into the parking area, I first saw the Emergency entrance, where they had rushed Waverly that fateful day. I felt a sickening feeling in my stomach and almost turned around to drive home.

Something pushed me onward. I parked the car, walked into the sterile lobby with the highly polished floors and the same two friendly receptionists whom I had seen before. I heard the location for the Grief Counseling, but before reaching my destination, I rushed to the bathroom to vomit. I washed my face, squared my shoulders and headed for the room. I told myself that I *could* do this!

When I scanned the persons assembled, I saw all Caucasian women, nearly all ten to fifteen years my senior. I couldn't possibly share my story with these women with whom I had nothing in common. I told myself that since it was awkward to leave, I would complete this first session and never return.

My Chaplain friend explained what we would glean from the six-week experience, after which she presented an "ice-breaker" exercise that forced each of us to pinpoint our respective levels of grief. Within an hour, all of us had cried more than once, hugged one or more persons at the session, and genuinely felt the pain of the others.

Age was irrelevant. Ethnic background was irrelevant. **Grief was grief!** It bonded us with the force of a group of persons on a combat mission in a faraway land. I was stunned at the speed and ease with which a dozen strange women shared the same sorrow!

The Chaplains would take us through the four phases of grief and bereavement (William Worden's *Grief Counseling and Grief Therapy Model*, 1991), the first of which was to *"accept the reality of the death of our loved one." "We must all accept the irreversibility of death and the fact that we won't see our loved ones again in this life."*

Before the Chaplain finished uttering those words, nearly all of us were reaching for tissues that were placed around the table at which we sat. I had intellectualized this truth, but hearing it spoken out loud made me feel so helpless. We all felt sad and lonely.

Then we heard these words: *"We'll learn how to retain a comforting image of our loved ones in our minds, but for right now, let those tears flow if you need to. It will get better, we promise."* The tears did flow, as we abandoned whatever was considered proper deportment. Someone gently squeezed a neighbor's arm, while another embraced the person next to her, until everyone helped everyone stop crying.

Thus, the first session was devoted to acknowledging the loss of someone we dearly loved and now lost. It was OK to feel confusion, anxiety, irritation, futility and panic, in conjunction with a lowering of our self-esteem, as we grappled with the reality of the situation. The important thing to remember was not to be preoccupied with death to the point of despair, which is a surrendering of our will to live. Not a good idea!

"Relocating the deceased" is what allows us to move on, which is the only option to climbing into the coffin with the deceased, or dying too soon of a broken heart. Those words gave us all a jolt of reality, since we were all there to learn how to go on living, not how to die!

The Chaplains validated each of our expressed feelings, while explaining that this was the normal first phase of the cycle of grief. I felt a silent guilt about thinking ill of people I knew were doing far less with their lives than my Waverly. Why hadn't God taken any of *them*?

Waverly and Ruth were an effective team for nearly five decades. We made a difference within our sphere of influence, gave time and treasure to countless persons, and lived Godly lives. Didn't that count towards longevity? I felt like I was half a person now, empty and isolated.

Others offered similar self-assessments of their immediate circumstance because they had been married around sixty years each. Someone's lower lip began to quiver, and we all recognized what would happen next. Within a relatively short time period, women who had recently met developed an intuitive sense about the well being of our comrades.

We surrounded the weakest person at that moment, and lifted her

41

spirits with our collective compassion. Some said they had been blindly obedient to their mates, and now felt completely lost living without them.

I offered the first bit of humor by saying that my obedience was never blind. I always had an "ulterior motive" to my submissive behavior. "Whenever I was 'busted' by my beloved, he'd say, *'Lucy, what have you dun?'* True, some of my schemes could have become comic skits for I Love Lucy television shows, but I believe that's what attracted Waverly to me. It's certainly what kept him staying with me!"

The first session was over too quickly, and all of us knew how others' respective loved ones had died. Being part of a bereavement group was what we all needed. The Spiritual Care Chaplains thanked us for such candid, passionate revelations about our families and our personal pain. They promised that continued attendance would bring comfort, support and encouragement, as we journeyed through the complex healing process. We hugged each other as we said goodbye.

Everyone showed up for the second session, smiling and offering warm greetings to the group. Despite generational differences, we had become what I affectionately called "The Grief Girls." I would never have believed this odd group of women would become closer in grief than we probably would have under happy circumstances.

The second of the four phases of grief was to *"process the pain of the grief."* The blunt reality was that each of us had to go through every part of the pain, from guilt to rage to depression and loneliness to trusting and healing. One woman said she felt abandoned by her deceased husband and by God. She admitted being bitter. Others quickly validated the need to lean on God at a time like this.

I reflected on my earliest feelings the moment Waverly died. I never resented God, but did question His reason for separating me from my partner of nearly half a century. Most of the Grief Girls were praying, church-going women who didn't go against God's authority. Still, there were no shortcuts to getting through this second phase of mourning. Being in a grief support group certainly helped us to corroborate our jumbled feelings, as we moved from disbelief and denial to acceptance of a "new normal" for our lives.

The Chaplains gently coaxed each participant to speak about the depth of our sorrow. There were displays of quiet tears and out-loud sobs, impromptu hugs, sharing of tissues, exhibiting good listening skills, and demonstrating genuine empathy among participants and the Chaplains. Surprisingly, we felt better after exposing our personal anguish.

Our Spiritual Care Chaplains gave us strategies to create positive images of our loved ones. We could prepare a scrapbook of memories from pictures depicting happy times together, or we could journal our feelings, even make a shrine somewhere in our homes, where we would place items having special meaning to our loved ones.

We learned that a journal was an effective tool to help us heal. It was a safe way to express and sort through our feelings, or relay our experiences with loved ones. For me, writing had always given me insight into the problem at hand. I used writing to work through a problem until I found an acceptable solution on the page before me.

I hadn't connected journaling to relieving stress before I went to Grief Counseling. *"Journal keepers pay attention to what's happened internally. Journaling allows sufficient introspection to relieve stress....It's a recording of how we process external experiences internally, and allows us to privately self-correct, if we deem correction necessary."*

Nothing we imagined to create was out of bounds, because the aim was to release the pressure that was pent up in the grieving persons. This exercise was purported to be a major first step on the path to personal healing.

I had already made a big scrapbook of memories, with most pictures coming from the collage my sister and friend assembled for the Home Going Celebration. I was also journaling my feelings every day, sometimes causing the ink on the page to bleed because of my tears. I couldn't picture erecting a shrine to Waverly in the house. Seeing his urn in a sunlit room was all I needed.

The Spiritual Care Chaplains went into more detail about the journaling. *"Start writing anywhere and let the pain and tears flow. It's cathartic, and you'll gain insight into your inner strengths and your ability to become self-sufficient. If you never had to be independent, you do now. Say farewell to some aspects of your previous life – in writing."* It made sense, and in fact, I could relate to the emotional release I felt while journaling.

My dilemma was whether or not to share my private feelings about my husband's death with even one other person. Surely my humorous mishaps would ease others' pain through laughter, so why not share the whole scope of my feelings? Maybe, but I was at a fragile point on my road to healing. I wasn't sure if I wanted the public to know everything about me.

Our Spiritual Care Chaplains revealed that the more difficult challenge would be to cease dwelling on the last days or hours of our loved ones, because focusing upon that image would slow the important recovery process. They added that we were being too hard on ourselves if we felt guilt over anything we said or did. *"You all made the best choices possible under difficult circumstances, and it's not fair or productive to second-guess yourselves when death or dying is at hand."* They were right, of course. But I was anxious to hear precisely how to stop my mind from beating up my heart.

They explained the importance of *"finding an enduring connection with the deceased in the midst of embarking on a new life."* It was expected that each of us would memorialize our mates, but the imperative was to move on with *our lives. "You must incorporate the essence of the deceased into new patterns of living."* That way, we'd become open to new relationships, new and healthy attachments.

I shared with the group that my whole adult life was spent with my mate, and I felt lost and unable to make decisions without his guidance. *"I cried when I realized I needed a professional tax service to do my taxes for the first time in my life. Waverly was a corporate tax specialist, so he always took care of that for us. He bought each of our four homes and more than a dozen cars, and he chose most of our vacation spots. He planned the menu and cooked our meals for the last decade. We had the same taste in everything, so I happily let him assume the lead in every area of my life except education, where I was the expert."* I could feel that stinging sensation behind my eyes, telling me I was about to cry again.

Whenever I've been anxious or afraid, it's been my pattern to interject humor into the situation to relax me. So I said, *"A year before my husband died, he was masterfully pressing buttons on remotes to choose a movie from the television, provide us with surround sound, and put the whole thing on pause until I made the popcorn.*

I joked that if he ever died before me, our house would be mute. Well, he died, and my home was silent until I learned to order a movie from the television, insert a DVD into the player, and play the stereos in three parts of the house, all with different remotes and gadgets. I CAN make good popcorn!" There was laughter and applause.

At our next session, the Spiritual Care Chaplains moved to the third phase of grief, *"to adjust to a world without the deceased."* One lady told how she and her husband would put fresh sheets on the bed each week. As she ran around the bed alone, trying to fit all four corners of the bottom sheet, it was too difficult to secure that last corner without the strength of her husband holding up one end of the mattress for her. She said she threw herself onto the unmade bed and burst into tears. Those nearby squeezed her hand to offer solace.

I volunteered how I felt the first time I made breakfast without cooking for two persons. There was one lonely egg in a pan, staring at me as if I should know that a second or third egg was missing. I threw the uncooked egg into the trash and cried into my coffee cup. I had to learn to cook for one person and eat the food I made, instead of tossing it because I was too depressed to eat. We discussed loss of appetite next. *"Grief causes vulnerability and discomfort."*

Another member at the session told us how she and her husband had danced at each anniversary for sixty-one years, and he died two days before they were to dance in celebration of sixty-two years together. She wanted one last dance that she could never have. My loss after forty-five years was no more or less unbearable than the loss this lady felt after sixty-one years. Widows will always want one more moment, or word, or caress from our mates, but we can't have more than God's plan allows. That's true in all situations of grief.

Our personal stories provided the perfect segue for the Chaplains to focus on the subject of loneliness. *"Anyone who's experienced grief knows the feeling of loneliness – the void we experience when we have loved someone and then lost that person."* We explored our related emotions of isolation, abandonment, indecisiveness and confusion. Would we ever get through a session without tissues and tears?

I was consoled when I heard that being afraid was a natural reaction to loneliness, because I really couldn't visualize a future apart from Waverly. I was fighting off depression every day, thinking I couldn't function well alone. Our Spiritual Care Chaplains assured us that loneliness, and then depression were necessary steps in the grieving process. The benefit to being alone was coming to terms with the areas in our lives where we needed to grow. I thought I needed growth everywhere!

"Listen, you'll seem to get better, then slip back into depression. Some of you will have a more difficult time the second year after your loved one has passed than you experienced the first year. Ask for your family's patience, without judgment or condescension." Wow, there was the real possibility of feeling worse during year two than we felt in this first year of bereavement? *"How could that be possible,"* I wondered?

We discussed in tearful detail how death makes us confront our own spirituality. The Chaplains suggested that sometimes we *should* embrace solitude. *"It's healthy to establish a 'prayer closet,' a special place where we go alone to restore ourselves, our relationships with others and our relationship with God."* It could be as large as a space in a room, or as small as a corner of the bathroom. The size of a prayer closet was not important. It was all about the intimacy with The Deity.

I had begun to pray on my knees every morning and evening since

Waverly died, but I never knew about establishing a prayer closet. I intended to create one in a corner of my clothing closet. It would be too painful to sit in his closet and talk to God because there were still many articles of clothing hanging, with his scent on them. I couldn't bring myself to part with them yet, although I'd already given a number of suits, coats and jackets, shoes and casual clothes away to relatives and friends who could wear them. I needed the security of keeping some of Waverly's clothes near me.

"You'll be developing a new sense of self without the identity of the relationship that is now gone. In time, you'll strengthen your self- esteem and sense of efficacy." The Chaplains suggested that we find new outlets for our creativity, join clubs or organizations, strengthen our faith, stay close to family and special friends.

"Don't be afraid to let your family and friends know how you're feeling at any moment. Don't shut them out because they're looking to you to guide them in how to comfort you. Don't push them away because you need and want their encouragement. Remember, they're grieving too, and at the same time, they're worrying about you."

I hadn't factored into my occasionally crestfallen existence the fact that those closest to me also loved Waverly and were dealing with their grief over his passing. My daughter and I frequently talked, but I had not asked my siblings or Waverly's how they were coping. I vowed to change that the moment the grief counseling session ended, and I did. My subsequent conversations with family members and close friends became candid, thoughtful and deliberate, with collective blessings following each dialogue. I began to see "the light at the end of the tunnel," though it was far off.

The fourth and last phase of grief involved "reinvesting emotional energy" to experience a sense of healing. Time was critical to this phase because we learned that, with time, tears will flow less often and we'll begin to remember only the pleasant aspects of the deceased. We will no longer blame ourselves for something missed or not done well enough. We'll begin to remember our loved ones with less pain in our hearts. Personal growth in our "new normal" living will afford us joy. We'll see that new opportunities lay ahead, and if we're wise, we'll "seize each day."

It's during this phase where grieving persons could expect to overcome feelings of guilt and betrayal. They would forgive themselves because they have suffered enough. They are ready to receive inner strength again by giving time and treasure to others. The importance of belief in a Higher Being can't be overstated. We must seek spiritual wellness.

Everyone agreed in principle that it was time to *"adjust to a world without the deceased on three levels: externally, internally and spiritually."* It was important for each Grief Girl to have a clear understanding of the role our loved one played in our lives, after which we could begin to develop a new sense of self-worth without the *"identity of that relationship."*

Additionally, we needed to accept that our circumstances were forever changed. There was no return to the past way of life. Lastly, it was healthy to create new goals, making adjustments about how we viewed the world from a spiritual perspective.

The Chaplains responded to a question about how we will know when we're getting better. *"You'll know you're better when you don't wake up thinking about your loved one, though you may reflect on your relationship at some point of every day. Time between bad periods will be longer, and you'll experience less guilt and anger. You'll find that you can plan and carry out new activities that you never would have undertaken if not for the reason you're grieving.*

Finally, you'll begin to fill the role vacated by your loved one, even if you don't do things exactly as he or she did them. Also, widows will notice that you are comfortable reinvesting in new relationships, which could include a romantic attachment down the road. Be open to all of it."

None of the Grief Girls had conquered the first phase, but we vowed to maintain contact with each other, to prop each of us up on anniversaries of the death of our mates, and to fellowship together bi-monthly. I offered my home for the first gathering, and we set a brunch date before ending Grief Counseling. We had become the kind of friends most folks hope to have once in their lifetime.

We planned monthly meetings at our respective homes or a local restaurant centrally located to all of us. We exchanged photos of our lost loves, but also of our current families. All the Grief Girls had nuclear and extended family support, which was just the right medicine to help us heal, as we got past the first stage of grieving and moved on to the next. None of us took for granted the huge benefit derived from having the presence and love of family around us.

The last thing we heard as the six-week course ended was, **"You don't get over grief – it gets over you!!"** Our helpful Spiritual Care Chaplains gave each of us *The Mourner's Bill of Rights* to keep and place in a prominent place in our homes. None of us thought grieving persons had "rights," until now:

The Mourner's Bill of Rights

1.   *You have the right to experience your own unique grief.*
2.   *You have the right to talk about your grief.*
3.   *You have the right to feel a multitude of emotions.*
4.   *You have the right to be tolerant of your physical and emotional limits.*
5.   *You have the right to experience "grief bursts."*
6.   *You have the right to make use of ritual.*
7.   *You have the right to embrace your spirituality.*
8.   *You have the right to search for meaning.*
9.   *You have the right to treasure your memories.*
10. *You have the right to move toward your grief and heal.*

Someone said, *"Time heals everything. So give time time.* **No matter how you feel, get up, dress up and show up. God will do the rest!"**

Grief Counseling helped me turn the corner, because now I corroborated what I was feeling and why. I had never heard of four phases of grieving, but after the six weeks of professional guidance, I had a blueprint against which to measure my progress in finding my "new normal" life.

I learned that when I "gave myself away" by allowing others access to the many talents God has bestowed upon me, I received the comfort I was desperately seeking. Who knew that selfless acts yielded self-help? Happiness! Peace! That's what I felt when I turned the mirror away from myself.

A dear friend and minister sent me some carefully chosen Biblical passages of particular significance to a grieving widow like me:

2 Samuel 1:17: *"David took up this lament concerning Saul and his son Jonathan." Expressing sorrow and finding words for grief over those who've gone to be with the Lord is healthy.*

John 11:25-27: *"Jesus said, "I am the resurrection and the life. The one who believes in me will live, even though they die." It is natural to mourn the loss of a loved one, but we can let Jesus hold us in His compassionate arms, knowing that he understands.*

1 Thessalonians 4:13-14: *"Brothers and sisters, we do not want you to be uninformed about those who sleep in death, so that you do not grieve like the rest of* *mankind, who have no hope. For we believe that Jesus died and rose again, and so we believe that God will bring with Jesus those who have fallen asleep in him."*

Revelation 21:4: *"He will wipe every tear from their eyes. There will be no more death or mourning or crying or pain, for the old order of things has passed away."*

When my son-in-law's Mom was grieving over the loss of her Mom, I sent her a CD of Ce Ce Wynans' song *You Will,* because I hoped her soothing words would offer my dear Sister a path to healing. I believe it did.

Recently, I played the song for myself, in hopes of receiving the same inspirational path to a day when I could be assured that I had begun to heal. It's a beautiful song with a perfect message to all of us who are going through the grieving process:

You Will, by Ce Ce Wynans

…Still I am not able to feel what you feel,
And I cannot say how long
It will take for you to heal,
But I believe you will, you will.
And someday, you'll find your smile again,
So take your time.
For time is what it's gonna to take,
And then one morning you'll awake
To find that one last tear. Oh, yes.
I believe you will.

The world has let you down,
And words that could explain cannot be found.
To say that I understand is not enough.
And it's gonna to be a little while
Before your heart will learn to trust,
But I believe it will, it will….

When you feel like all your hope is gone,
Keep holding on,
'Till you find your way back to the Garden,
Find a way to give your heart again.
And I know your broken heart will mend,
*I **know** it will….*

49

And you will find your smile again,
So take your time.
For time is what it's gonna to take,
And then one morning you'll awake
To find that one – last – tear! Oh, yes.

And you'll heal.
I believe you will.

Chapter Eight
Handling the "Firsts" with Grace in Pain

THUS SAITH THE LORD: *"When thou passest through the waters, I will be with thee; and through the rivers, they shall not overflow thee: when thou walkest through the fire, thou shalt not be burned; neither shall the flame kindle upon thee."*
Isaiah 43:2

A chunk of time during Grief Counseling was devoted to accepting how difficult special days can be after someone we love passes. Somewhere in the literature we received, it said, *"Since love does not end with death, special days may result in a renewed sense of personal grief…a feeling of loss unlike that experienced in the routine of daily living."*

The recommendation was to take one day at a time, feeling no remorse for any decisions we would make while handling the "firsts." It was also good to hear that whatever we decided to do each special day of the first year after our loved one passed, might be handled differently the second year. *"Remind yourself that your feelings are normal and temporary... and your needs may legitimately change from day to day."*

I was glad to put some terminology to my ambivalent feelings about the grief process, embarrassingly surprised to realize that grief has no end date. But attending Grief Counseling sessions led by trained Spiritual Care Chaplains let me know I wasn't alone and I wasn't grieving improperly.

That said, I hadn't anticipated the range of emotions that would surround me on each special day during the first year after Waverly's passing. At the funeral, actually throughout the whole weekend leading up to the Home Going Celebration, I sensed that every eye was on me. Was I eating, sleeping, crying, or staring into the distance? Did I need anything? Many persons tried to comfort me with stories about the loss of their loved ones, or by saying that my husband was *"in a better place now, in perfect health, without any pain."*

I found myself engaging in light conversations designed to let folks know I would eventually be OK. But as bits of laughter emerged from hearing my siblings recall funny situations into which I got myself, I noticed that I was laughing, too – at ME! I felt that by being open to candid, plentiful expressions of humor and grief, I could make it through the first year as a widow, with grace, albeit in pain.

A big takeaway from the Grief Counseling for me was to let others know how I'm feeling at any given time, instead of shutting out people who sincerely wanted to help me. *"Grieving is nature's way of healing the mind and heart from the greatest injury of all. Allow yourself the privilege of limping until your wounds have healed and you can learn to run again."* I began communicating my needs, my fears and my desires, which was a large step in putting those closest to me at ease.

One of my dearest friends returned home after spending a full week with me after the funeral. It was at that point that I began to experience uneasy sleeping at night. Mornings were tough, too, as I rolled from my side of the bed to Waverly's, wanting to feel him lying next to me. Feeling Lucky's paw pushed into my side as she snored was little substitute for Waverly's gentle caress, but it would have to do.

At the two-week mark since Waverly died, I felt like posting something on the funeral website, below his obituary and picture:

"Overall, I feel OK, not depressed too often or sad too much. But it's hard cooking for one, eating alone, sleeping alone. There's too much food in the refrigerator, it takes too long to get enough dirty clothes for a laundry load, and I've stopped running the dishwasher because it takes a week to fill. My folding and ironing is diminished, and there's nothing fresh to place in his drawers or hang in his closet.

Waverly always insisted on using china and silverware, so I won't resort to using paper plates. Besides, he could be watching, in which case I would expect to hear an unfavorable whisper in the air. When I pull into the driveway, I look for him and Lucky to be sitting in the garage waiting for me. Our two lawn chairs are still where he left them."

Why did I write that? Before I knew it, I had left the computer and was wailing into a bathroom towel. I stopped the tears and returned to the website to finish my post.

"Since age nineteen, I haven't eaten or slept alone more than a dozen times, which I know is an enormous gift to have had. But it's taking time for me to adapt to less joy in my immediate surroundings. Though I'm grateful for the love of an extraordinary number of family members and great friends, I need to learn to wipe away tears sooner and be more productive each day. I want to be grateful for all that I have, instead of lamenting my fate. Today WILL be a good day."

I used to prepare big meals, especially when everyone came to our home for Sunday dinner. It was now pointless to cook a full dinner daily, but I didn't want to eat less than balanced meals at each sitting either. The compromise was to make meals big enough to last me three days. In keeping with Waverly's standards in food presentation, served on china, I forced myself to delight in placing dinner on the plate in an appealing way. Looked like something in a restaurant, and Waverly

52

would be proud of me. I said the blessing and ate dinner in front of the television, so I'd have some noise around me. I used real utensils and placed a linen napkin in my lap, but I skipped adding the dinner candle to my snack tray!

On the second day of eating that big meal, I put everything into a bowl, and may have used a big spoon instead of a knife and fork. By the third day, whatever was left of the meal became a sandwich served on a china bread plate. I had overcome my first dilemma of how to cook meals for more than a day, and eat them alone.

Memorial Day was the first family gathering after Waverly's death in March. It had been scheduled at my house for months, but I was apprehensive about how I would feel at the first barbecue where Waverly wasn't the "grill master." My brother stepped up to do the grilling, and everyone brought enough food to feed my neighborhood. We ate, drank and swam in the pool. I felt happy by day's end, just like old times. Contentment turned to exhaustion, just like old times. I slept well that night.

Someone asked if I felt Waverly's presence or dreamed about him. I said I hadn't. I had, however, felt a calm all around me while at home, and wasn't overwhelmed by the large spaces in my home. I felt safe, not ready to consider moving to a smaller accommodation yet.

Then close to the time that I awoke one morning, I had my first dream about Waverly. I saw him wearing a cream, collard short-sleeved shirt with small green triangles on it like little Christmas trees. It wasn't one of the dozens of shirts I had in his closet. He looked like he did before he died, glasses and all, and I noticed that he had lost some weight. I hugged him hard, smiling as I praised him for having a smaller stomach.

Instantly, he vanished from my arms. I didn't see him walk away, nor did I know anything about my appearance, but I awoke feeling happy about my first dream about my "Darling Forever." Within minutes, I found myself sobbing because I remembered the security I always felt while in his strong arms. I enjoyed that tight embrace in the dream, and it was gone when I awoke. I chose to treasure the dream more than the sadness that followed, and I looked forward to my next dream about Waverly, no matter how long the wait.

Shortly after the funeral, my three siblings living in Florida vowed that we would get together monthly, rather than waiting for the major holidays and spending only a short time together at each big event. *"Life's too short, as we've seen with my brother-in-law's passing,"* my brother said.

I offered to host our first fun night – dinner and a movie. Before everyone arrived, I made it a point to learn how to rent a movie from the television, and to hear that movie in "surround sound." Yes, I was quite proud of myself for figuring that out without a manual. I made sandwiches and dessert, and we had wine and sodas and snacks. I was excited about having company and noise in the house again, so soon after Memorial Day.

We all read the trailers from recent movies, and on first blush, the movie *We Bought a Zoo*, starring Matt Damon seemed to be a comedy. I knew that my brother and sisters were being extra careful to choose a movie to make me laugh, not cry. We ordered that movie. It was funny at first, watching this family relocate to a zoo, to live and manage the animals and expansive property.

But within a few minutes, we saw that the main character had lost his wife, and he was trying to accept a great loss by moving his family to a zoo. There were references to how much he loved his wife, and flashbacks to times they had spent together.

In a few tender scenes, he revealed his vulnerability and sadness since her passing. I could feel all peripheral eyes on me, with my siblings still hoping they had chosen an up-beat movie that wouldn't upset me.

I kept it together until the end, when Matt told his family how he met his wife and how they were meant to be together from that moment forward. He flashed back to their first meeting at a diner, and took the audience and his family from joy to tears within minutes. What a great actor!

As the movie ended, everyone was weeping at the main character's loss of his one true love, but I was wailing. I had buried my face in my hands, trying to avoid the flood of tears and loud cries that followed. The harder I tried to stop, the louder and the more I cried.

My sister quickly made a joke about the "excellent" movie choice we all had made, and how you can't always tell the plot from the trailer. I left the room to wash my face. I rested my head against the bathroom mirror, and whispered through the last tears I intended to shed that evening, *"I miss you, Honey. I don't know how to go on without my Darling Forever. Everyone is trying so hard to help me stop grieving, but everything I hear and see comes back to you and me!"*

When I returned to my siblings, they stopped talking at the same time. They were, no doubt, wondering what to do to cheer me up before they all left. I put their collective minds at ease by spouting some of the Grief Counseling terms about there being no right or wrong way to grieve, nor is there an end to grieving. I would be fine in time.

"Don't worry when I cry because it's always better to let it out than keep it inside. You've comforted me from the moment you learned of Waverly's death, so when I cry like this, you must know it will pass. See, it's passed one more time because I'm no longer crying, right?"

I kissed and hugged my three siblings, and they left. I didn't cry any more that evening, instead, thanking God for the best siblings a woman could wish to have. Around that time, my older brother in New York and my brother-in-law in New Jersey were calling every day to check on me. I knew I was *"blessed and highly favored."*

It was mid-July before I knew it. Waverly had been gone from me four months, and I received a beautiful invitation from the Spiritual Care Chaplains at the hospital where he had died. They had an annual "Patients' Service of Remembrance," held in the hospital chapel to give honor to all the special persons who had died during the previous year.

I wasn't sure I was ready to attend such a memorial because my feelings were still raw and I cried at some point during every day. Then I read the message at the bottom of the invitation, and felt compelled to attend in support of MY loved one:

"Those we invite to weave upon the tapestry of our lives
Bring beauty and design that we enjoy and even adopt as
our own. And though a person who is part of our tapestry dies,
In our hearts forever is what they have lovingly sewn."

This was my first time returning to the hospital since Waverly died. My mouth was dry and my palms moist. I had already parked the car, so I talked to myself the entire time I walked into the hospital, and down the long corridor to the door of the chapel. I had passed that door twice daily for the six days my darling was in the hospital, never stopping to kneel in prayer before taking the elevator up to his room.

No time for regrets about that, since my lower lip was already quivering as I entered the sanctuary. The room filled quickly, and the program began with prayer. On the big screen in front of us were the names of all persons the hospital staff considered "weavers on the tapestry of our lives" within one year.

As each name was called, the family members present were asked to come forward to receive a small token of love in remembrance of the deceased. I was shaken when I saw "Waverly Lee Baskerville, Jr." appear in large, bold letters on the screen. His name remained there until I received my gift and returned to my seat.

As soon as I sat down, Waverly's full name dissolved under the wings of a graceful white dove that flew away before my eyes. The screen was blank for a second, until the Chaplains acknowledged the next loved one and family. I felt incomplete, wanting to follow the dove until Waverly could emerge from underneath the wing to make me feel whole again.

I realized that seeing that white dove carrying Waverly's name away was symbolic for carrying him away to Heaven. But my heart was again shattered, and I could hardly contain my sobbing so that others could hear their loved ones' names being called. I buried my head in my lap. Someone reached under my arm and placed a stack of tissues near my face. The person squeezed my shoulder and left me.

I pulled myself together in the midst of others acting the same way I did. A soloist sang, followed by choir music and refreshments. As good as the coffee smelled, I couldn't eat or drink at that moment. I needed fresh air and to clear my mind on the ride back home. I wasn't glad I had come at first, but by the time Lucky greeted me back home, I was convinced I had done the right thing.

It was the middle of April, five weeks after Waverly's death, when I joined the "State Writers' Guild." I was a first-time author, eager to be part of this large network of authors, poets, editors and publishers.

That was a few months back, and here I was looking at an invitation to the Annual Writers' Conference in mid-October. Waverly would have wanted me to go to listen to the keynote speaker, attend the all-day workshops, and mingle with other authors. He was very proud that I finished my first book of four hundred, fifty-nine pages in five months, and that the only publisher to whom we sent the manuscript accepted it with little editing.

I awoke that Saturday morning with mixed feelings. I was excited about venturing into the world of professional writing, imparting and gleaning knowledge about our craft, and taking lots of notes. The day promised to be chocked full of breakout sessions about writing, publishing and editing, with meaningful networking over our meals.

Unhappiness overcame me as I dressed, because I had taken every step towards becoming an author, with Waverly at my side. He was the mastermind who distilled whatever information I brought to him, and offered my next step. I knew I would miss that, as well as the exciting conversation we would have had when I got home.

Limiting the tears I shed, I dressed, put the directions to the writer's conference into my GPS (by myself!), and went on to my first State Writers' Guild event. I had a great day, filled with rich discussions, serious networking with peers and a delicious breakfast and lunch.

But, while driving home, water filled my eyes *again* because my Darling wouldn't be there to hear about my day. I didn't realize I was crying until the water rested on my neck. Why didn't I feel it running from my eyes to my cheeks to my chin, and finally to my neck? Why couldn't I stop it?

I knew I would be opening the garage to find the two empty lawn chairs we always sat on, and once inside the house, I would eat a silent dinner. I needed to move those chairs, or put them out of my view to avoid contributing to my depression by walking past two empty lawn chairs to get to the back door. *"Tomorrow,"* I thought!

Instead of allowing myself to whimper when I came into the house, I *told* myself to appreciate how good it was to be greeted by Lucky, demanding food and a walk. I thought about how blessed I was to have my daughter and son-in-law come twice during the day, just to take care of Lucky for me.

I called Alicia to share my day, and she was enthusiastic about everything I said. It was a "close second" to telling it all to Waverly, and I enjoyed my dinner more. Signs were all around to teach me to strike the balance between loneliness and happiness.

Alicia called me back after dinner to direct me to the garage again. What had I missed seeing when I came home? I was so focused on the chairs that I didn't notice that to the left of the chairs were six large boxes filled with my first novel, *HOODLESS KLAN*. Alicia and Bruce had met my publisher earlier in the day, picked them up, and dropped them off in my garage to surprise me. They took the tops off of the boxes, so that I saw twenty-four shiny book covers with my picture and full name on each. It made my heart race with exhilaration.

For the first time, I accepted the real prospect of being a published author. I sat in one of the lawn chairs and broke down. I was overwhelmed by the direction my life was taking without Waverly.

I felt nervous about the nasty folks around whom this fiction work was based, but excited for the virtuous folks to read about the characters they inspired. Not one book was sold yet, but I had come this far in just a few months!

Despite putting my elbows in my lap and my head in my hands to cry, I had the presence of mind not to let a tear fall on any of those new books!! Waverly and I used to acknowledge the fact that we'd had "quite a ride" together to that point in our lives, most of it at warp speed. Seems I was still traveling at that speed since he left me, no doubt by his and God's design to help me cope with my huge loss!

I shared the good news with my pastor. His wife sent me a message that evening. *"Wow, Dr. Ruth. I can only imagine what you are experiencing right now, the excitement, but also the longing for your beloved husband to share it with you. So you go ahead and let the tears flow. God is keeping them in His bottle and they are precious to Him right now. He is going to use your book to bring hope and healing to others, I truly believe. We pray you'll be the bestselling author you are destined to be!! Feel my hugs and love."* I was encouraged, indeed.

At the time of my retirement, after forty-two years in education, I was a charter school principal in a suburban district out-of-state. My four-year ordeal at the hands of some treacherous, powerful people governed by racial bias, had left me emotionally drained. Once safely back home and far away from those people, my dear Waverly convinced me to journal my feelings as a way to heal my mind.

However, once he read some of my work, he insisted that I had the beginning of a novel and should dedicate myself to writing it. We spent every day and night together, reading, writing, eating and enjoying each other's company without my having to leave for events or meetings. Waverly guarded my calendar! My untimely retirement, at the time an unwelcomed action, was in reality God's mercy in giving us quality time before He took Waverly almost one year later.

It was Waverly who chose the only publisher to whom we submitted my manuscript, and the morning he died, we read the email together about my book being accepted for publication. He had read every word of it, and now he knew that his wife was on a path to become a published author.

In the midst of grieving, I scheduled two out-of-state book signings, both of which proved to be financially successful. I was traveling and expanding my "platform" of supporters without my mate and best friend to coach me. It was exciting, unnerving and bittersweet, but I learned to maneuver through airports and drive rented cars, set my own schedule, and find contentment as a single woman-author.

At the same time, I was often gripped by loneliness and a deep sense of loss. I wanted to tell Waverly what I'd been doing, ask his advice about my future, share conversation over a meal and hear him say he was pleased that I was accomplished and busy, despite missing him with all my heart. The reality was I couldn't do any of those things. My future as an author would be mine alone to determine.

My brother-in-law, who was the last person to speak to Waverly outside of me, called to relay his first dream about his oldest brother. He posted it on the funeral website to share with others who were writing and reading posts about Waverly:

"My dear brother, I'm so happy to say that I had a dream about you! It was so real. We didn't speak, but you hugged me like my Big Brother and made me feel like a little boy again! You smiled at me to let me know you're OK! It's three months since you left us to go to a better place. Tell Mama and our brother, Sherman that I miss them. Love, you. Baby Brother."

I mentioned earlier that Waverly was an organ and tissue donor, and in the fall, The Organ & Tissue Donation Institute held its annual scrapbooking and quilting meeting for donor families. It was my first time attending, and my siblings and daughter joined me, along with my grandchildren.

I needed that moral support, too, once family members of donors shared intimate details of how loved ones died and how much they missed their partner, parent, child or sibling. Also in attendance were organ transplant recipients, grateful for the "gift of life." Beyond tearful storytelling, our task was to choose from a plethora of crafts provided, in order to create a nine-inch quilt square representing the essence of our deceased loved ones.

I thought of the Broadway play, *Rent*, and the song asking how to measure one year in our lives. How would I ever describe Waverly's full life in a square space that small? My family helped me choose a burgundy fabric for the background, and gold braiding for the border. That covered the "regal" part of Waverly.

We reviewed the fifteen pictures I brought, to select the ones encompassing his family, career, interests, all surrounding his picture, which went in the center of the square. We had to have "Darling Forever" at the top, his birth and death, which we called "sunrise" and "sunset." Chosen pictures included his parents, his daughter at her birth and on her wedding day, he and I, he and our dog, Lucky, his baby brother on his wedding day, the grandchildren after a ballet recital, the famous Wall Street bull representing his career, and his lemon chiffon, 1978 Silver Shadow II Rolls Royce.

At the bottom of the quilt square, I wanted to acknowledge the five college friends who stayed together for forty-seven years and became the BFFFFs (Best Friends Forever From Fredonia). I listed our five first names in alphabetical order across the bottom of the quilt square. Waverly was the baby of the group, being born in the last month of the year of all our births.

I believe Waverly would have approved of the finished product, which was one of thirty-two personalized squares hand-stitched onto a large mural. Several murals capturing the lives of deceased persons would regularly accompany The Organ & Tissue Donation Institute staff, as they traveled to events to urge individuals to "give the gift of life."

Tears came and stopped, and came again while we were looking at pictures and colored fabric and ribbons and cutout letters. It had been my experience that crying early in the day set the tone for a full day of weeping. My daughter and siblings had the same experience, but by day's end, we finished an elegant tribute to Waverly Lee Baskerville, Jr. We fit everything tastefully into the space allotted on the square, and submitted it to be hand-stitched onto a mural.

Before I realized it, we were into November, and with it came what would have been our forty-fifth anniversary. Thankfully, my daughter and her family insisted on helping me decorate the house for the holidays. It was a brilliant idea because my focus was forward, towards a happy and celebratory occasion. That took my focus off of bereavement, at least for most of my anniversary day.

The next day was Waverly Baskerville, Sr.'s 90th birthday, and his youngest son planned a party for him. I flew to New Jersey for a book signing and Pop's party. Everyone in attendance made a toast to Pop's namesake, who none expected to die before his father. The celebration was grand, although there were a few tears from some of the guests and me.

Once again, promoting my book helped ease the pain associated with my first anniversary without my mate. Visiting my father-in-law for his birthday gave me special comfort, as we reminisced about Waverly's childhood before he met me, and a host of stories about our family times together.

Was it December already? It had been nine months since Waverly died, and this was his birthday month. My daughter's family entertained me once again, and my pastor and his wife had me over for dinner soon after. Besides doing happy things to keep my mind off of the sad reality, I was tutoring five students between elementary and high school ages. What a joy it was to teach again!

At the beginning of the Christmas holiday season, I spent the evening with my daughter, son-in-law and grandchildren. We made cookies. My granddaughters each broke an egg on the table before I broke the one that went into the batter, and we baked and decorated the cookies.

We shared a delicious meal, and I commented that my appetite was always good when I had loving people with whom to share the meal. I doubted that I would ever become comfortable eating alone, hearing myself chew because there was no jovial conversation going on. I wrapped presents and helped trim their tree. I really had a great time.

When I got home, I noticed that Alicia had slipped a card into my purse, full of glitter that spilled all over my wallet. It was a very tender card for a "Special Mother." The words were simply beautiful. Despite my happy disposition, I burst into tears because this was the first special card that didn't come "to both of you" from dear Alicia and Bruce. I had to accept the harsh reality that future celebratory cards would be directed only to me. That was a painful "first" for both Alicia and me.

I wanted to call to thank her for all the words she wrote about me under the already touching sentiments printed on the card. But I rationalized that she dropped it into my purse to keep from weeping. I waited, composed myself, and then made the call to thank her, without shedding a tear.

She was having a hard time thinking of this holiday season without Daddy, but she was glad she and I had begun a spiritual connection. I drank a glass of water to keep from crying again, and told her I, too, was finding it hard to shop, send Christmas cards with just my signature, and plan our gathering on Christmas Day without having Waverly to talk through all the plans with me.

Soulful Christmas songs had been our favorite, but we especially enjoyed Handel's *Messiah* while we cooked Christmas dinner every year. Waverly always made his famous sweet potato and apple pies, helped me slice and dice vegetables, and carved the big turkey at the table.

I ended our conversation by saying, "Tomorrow will be another day, another chance to 'get it right' by doing something important to someone else. It's the only way to ease our separate and collective pain, Angel (my nickname for my daughter)."

Gee, I missed my partner, who always planned the best holiday menus and purchased the best holiday gifts for everyone. He was the consummate host, which is why everyone loved coming to our home all the time. He was known for keeping the fire in the fireplace blazing, and for keeping everyone's glass full. He cooked, carved, and distributed piles of presents to everyone in our home, all while keeping the music filling the air throughout the day.

I got excited about cooking Christmas dinner and having all that jubilant noise in my house from siblings, kids and grandchildren, and one neighbor. I had decorated inside and outside like I did when Waverly was here. All the palm trees and shrubs donned sparking, bright white lights. I had garland around the doors, with lights chasing the green garland everywhere. Big, lighted wreaths hung from the double doors in the front of the house. The four, lighted pillars at the entrance to our property were inviting, as well.

Inside, I hung over one hundred Christmas cards on the pillars that separated the living from the dining room, placed holiday ornaments and lights around the lanai, the fire place and the balcony.

The magnificent staircase, curving to the right and left at the first landing, had garland, lights, and red bows wrapped around almost all the space on the banister. Big toy soldiers stood at attention on different steps of the staircase. Had a fire inspector shown up, this would have been called a safety hazard, but since only I was scrutinizing my decorated staircase, it simply looked breathtaking!

My grandchildren put bows and garland on every knob and object on which something could hang, and the house looked like a curiosity shop right out of Dickens. We put lights on trees and around the front door, candles in all thirty-two windows, lighted candy canes around the front walkway, Santa hats on every object in my home with a head.

Waverly used to kid me about the thousands of lights I put up each year. He would say, *"Lucy, now airplanes can land in our town without an airport because YOU supplied the lighted airstrip!"* Naturally, I'd ignore the comment. Waverly knew that I put white lights on every tree and bush around our property, so there was no need to call me *"Lucy." No need at all!*

The Family Services Coordinator from The Organ & Tissue Donation Institute sent me this note: *"You made it through the holiday! Although what you've been through is devastating, you're able to grieve in a healthy way by expressing your feelings openly. You are such a wonderful example for your grandchildren!! I give you so much credit, and I hope that you also give yourself the same!"*

New Year's Eve was my first time being home alone on a holiday or celebration day since Waverly died. My parents used to say that if you bring the New Year in on a dirty house, or with dirty clothes in the hamper, you had bad luck throughout the next year. We kids believed it, and rushed to have everything clean and washed by the time midnight came. As we banged pot tops together to make noise befitting a brand New Year, we praised each other for avoiding bad luck in the New Year.

In retrospect, I think the parents used some clever psychology to get us to clean our rooms. Regardless, the habit was formed, and will be with me until I die. I finished shopping and making sure the house was perfect for the New Year by 7:00 p.m., and then cried when there was nothing left to do. I told myself that I couldn't whimper for five hours until they rang in the New Year in New York City. So I stopped, just like that.

I had mixed emotions about watching people hugging and kissing at midnight, but I felt a quiet calm when the hour struck, and I raised a glass of wine to every happy couple. I thanked God for more years of happiness and excitement than I deserved in my lifetime, and asked for Him to reveal His vision for me in 2013. He must be still pondering His response!

The New Year at my church meant that the congregation would engage in its annual prayer and fasting to inspire a good and prosperous year ahead. The *HOLY BIBLE* often linked prayer with fasting, to bring about change or spiritual growth.

I had never fasted. This group chose to do the twenty-one day *"Daniel Fast,"* patterned after the *Book of Daniel.* When the evil king insisted that Daniel and other captors eat food that was raised up to pagan gods for blessings, Daniel refused to eat it. He had favor with one of the prison guards, who allowed him to have fruits, vegetables and water, exclusively. He thrived on the sparse food selection because his God was supreme.

There's more to the story, but I was stuck on the limited variety of foods *we* could eat. It was hard for me to grasp the concept that by denying ourselves food, while praying and reading the *HOLY BIBLE* more often, we would draw closer to God.

My first long prayer was to ask God to make the twenty-one days go quickly. The fast would end on Super Bowl Sunday, and I was invited to a party where there was sure to be an abundance of decadent foods and desserts to please every palate. I needed to focus on the fast and not the Super Bowl party, but how could I do that?

My pastor and his wife guided me in taking the spiritual path I intended to follow with fidelity. We were partners, encouraging each other to stay faithful to the end, in order to receive whatever *"good and perfect gift"* God would deliver to His followers.

The first day of the fast, my head hurt so badly from the absence of caffeine in my body that I was too dizzy to stand for a couple of hours. Lucky and I took a nap because I was also too dizzy to kneel in prayer without falling over. Who said, *"This, too, shall pass,"* and why had that quote popped into my dizzy head in the first place?

I had the hang of it by the third day, but all I could think about was the day I would have a bacon and egg sandwich on a roll, and a hot cup of coffee for breakfast. For these twenty-one days, I was eating raw, then cooked vegetables and fruits for breakfast!

Would seasoning the seven or eight food items we could eat really have cost me a blessing from God? I was too much of a coward to find out, so I used three bottles of *Mrs. Dash* seasoning, searching for anything I could call *"tasty!"*

My pastor's wife knew how to use natural ingredients to create a hybrid breakfast biscuit and a soy patty that vaguely resembled a hamburger. It wasn't! I remember saying, "Trying to emulate Jesus is just too hard! How can I be this hungry and speak only positive words into the atmosphere? I don't understand spiritual warfare, and my impatience and temper keep warring with my kind nature. The *Daniel Fast* book said *thoughts* count, too, right? Oh, No! Could this invalidate my fast?"

At the two-week mark, I was ready to give up and run to the nearest fast food establishment. Increased prayer and my pastor's cooking kept my "eyes on the prize," and I felt like I was spiritually sprinting during every day of that last week of fasting and praying.

At the conclusion of my first and only fast to date, I had lost ten pounds, and actually felt closer to God than at any time in my life. We determined that it was successful in our personal lives, as well as a boost for the spiritual growth of the church.

Right after we said our last prayers ending the fast without once cheating, we turned our attention to the Super Bowl Sunday party, where the Devil made us fill our plates to overflowing. We ate it all, and didn't get sick either!

When Valentine's Day arrived, Alicia noted that this was the last "first" since Daddy died. Wow! We made it through nearly a full year since he passed. When I walked Lucky, Waverly used to call from the balcony, holding a cup of coffee, *"Hello, Beautiful."* Valentine's Day reminded me of how much I missed the unimportant chatter between life partners throughout the day, as well as the surprise gifts that came my way, particularly on Valentine's Day.

I had spent my whole life with either my family or my mate, never having a single woman's life until Waverly died. Now, every once in awhile, I look up at the empty balcony, thinking, *"Being without Waverly just sucks!"*

As I approached the anniversary of the ten days before he died, I relived the day Waverly asked me to call "911," and discovered in the hospital emergency room that he had dangerously low levels of sodium. They admitted him, and he stayed for six days.

Twice during his stay, he woke up in a panic and took off all the monitoring devices. He was moving around the hospital room searching for me. He could hear me, but couldn't find me. I jokingly reminded him that the reason he couldn't find me was that I was home sleeping with Lucky.

He needn't have worried because I would be back every day, twice a day. His skin and eyes were bright, and I felt confident he was getting better. During physical therapy, he stretched those colored elastic bands so far across his chest, or from his ankle to his chin, that the therapist holding one end was lifted off her feet!

That's another reason it was hard for me to accept that after being home only two nights and one day, he would die. At least he got to come home and sleep in his bed next to me both nights.

I took stock of my life over the past year. I'd gotten my first novel published and sold nearly five hundred copies. I had attached myself to a community center providing fine and performing arts to some of our most under-served children, and coached some dropouts to pass the GED. I successfully tutored five other students, all of whom passed their grade level or college entrance tests. These were paying clients, so our collective accomplishment put ME out of a tutoring job!

My spiritual faith had grown exponentially from the previous year. Not only was I praying twice daily, but I was also reading my *HOLY BIBLE* daily and attending Bible Study and church regularly. My family said I was morphing into a self-reliant woman of faith, while getting used to being a widow. I was becoming more patient and tolerant, less judgmental, a beautiful "butterfly." Everyone noticed. All their words of praise made me wonder what my disposition must have been like as a "caterpillar."

Despite reading all the scriptures, I was just learning about the difference between the natural and spiritual realms of being. Elevated to the bottom step of the spiritual ladder, I was convinced that *someone* had written a *new HOLY BIBLE* while I slept! After all, I had read it and could recite all sixty-six books by heart!

For the first time, the stories and parables throughout the book caused me to focus on what's really important in my life. It's about connections and communication, not tangible things that we leave behind when we transition.

It was a week before the anniversary of Waverly's passing, and I awoke agitated, nervous. Right after reading the scripture that my baby sister sent me daily, I saw this email from The Organ & Tissue Donation Institute Community Outreach person:

"It is perfectly OK for you to feel lost, and reminisce about where you were a year ago. Do not put pressure on yourself to have perfect days, and even good days

65

all of the time! Embrace your tears and your mourning for the loss of your darling husband! Waverly was an amazing man, and I'm so glad your faith is strong and you're able to find some peace. But one year is truly only a short time, and you have the right to wonder why, and to wish things could have been different.

You are strong enough to move forward. Let your family embrace you this weekend and love on you because you are deserving of it, and many of them miss him so deeply as well. It may be healing for them to support you sometimes, so please let them. This will also help you smile and laugh more truly when those emotions come as well! Giant hugs, Dr. Ruth! You are an inspiration to us at the Institute."

Exactly four days before the one-year mark of Waverly's death, the Organ & Tissue Donation Institute sponsored a fun day for donor families. I was asked to be Co-Chairperson of the event, and my idea of a day without tears was to copy the game *Candyland*, setting up "sweets stations" in the large room where the event was to be held. At each station was something sweet to eat or fun to do for the whole family.

There were stations for popcorn and cotton candy, a chocolate fountain, cookie decorating, face painting, balloon making, and more. Being the wise old senior member of the planning committee, I set up a coffee station where adults could come and relax in a "quiet" area over a fresh, hot cup of coffee. That was the station to which I assigned myself. Someone had to do it!

Twenty of my family members and close friends came to Candyland to support me. I was REALLY glad that, when my oldest grandson told me he had four cotton candy cones, my grandchildren didn't live with me! No, they were going home with their parents! Needless to say, "a good time was had by all."

I wondered how I would feel on the morning of March 13th, expecting to cry a lot. It was exactly one year since Waverly passed away. I was weepy, but never altered my busy schedule. Before I knew it, evening had come and I had a productive day. Waverly would have wanted that, since he pushed me to make every day a fruitful one.

He also taught me the importance of never giving in to grief, despite shedding unavoidable tears. *"Suck it up, Honey,"* he used to say about something with which I was dealing. That night, I was reading the book *Profiting from Trials*. The very first words were these: **James 1:2-8:** *"My brethren, **count it all joy** when you fall into various trials, knowing that the testing of your faith produces patience. But let patience have its perfect work, that you may be perfect and complete, lacking nothing...."*

I received a number of cards and phone calls from those thinking about me on the anniversary of Waverly's death. I also opened some e-cards of sympathy. Perhaps a goal for me this second year as a widow should be to learn to send an e-card. I made a comprehensive list of the changes in my life within one year, nearly all of them completely different from what I thought I knew about myself and where I thought I was going. Creating and sending an e-card would start my "bucket list"!

I decided to keep the *HOLY BIBLE* strapped to my hip, so when I felt sorrow overtaking me, I could reach for it like "blazing guns" and annihilate that depression. Good plan, right? I kept my focus on my "new normal," rather than to long for my old life again. That, plus two full glasses of wine caused me to sleep peacefully on March 13th.

The next day, I had on my calendar to attend a lunch given by the Spiritual Care Chaplains from the hospital where Waverly died. I had seen the "Grief Girls" four times since Grief Counseling sessions ended, and all of us were going to the luncheon – in the cafeteria at the hospital.

We talked by phone that morning, and were happy to be getting together again with the professionals who showed us how to push past the pain that gripped us at the start of the first weekly help sessions. All the Grief Girls had bought my first book, and wanted to share their thoughts with me about that, too.

The sun was shining, the air brisk. By God's grace, I had another chance to "get it right." I intended to grab hold of each blessing with every one of my polished nails. It promised to be a special, upbeat day for all of us.

Our Chaplains said we were among the best Group Counseling participants because we developed trust among ourselves at the first grief session, and kept in touch when counseling ended. I brought tissues to the luncheon, just in case.

Each of us was asked to describe our lives since Group Counseling ended. Maybe because we had already spent time together crying, none of us wept. I counted myself among widows with the most personal fulfillment in life.

The following Sunday, the first anniversary of Waverly's Home Going Celebration, I took a long look at the beautiful morning sky. I headed to church to say a special, quiet thanks to God for walking beside me throughout the first year of my being a grieving widow.

I planned to have dinner with Alicia and family, always a huge comfort to me. I would end the day writing another chapter in my second book, about the many hilarious situations into which I had gotten myself while trying to **"be"** Waverly.

Months before mid-April, my BFFFFs from college had convinced me to take a cruise to the Southern Caribbean with them. I was the only one who had never been on a cruise. Naturally, I wished Waverly were going with us.

At first our set-sail date was far off, and then it was tomorrow! All of us had our respective suitcases on the bedroom floor, with clothes strewn all over the bed and chairs until each outfit was fully accessorized. I made the suggestion that we should fully accessorize the outfits we knew we wouldn't get to wear on the cruise! Excitement was building, and I felt genuinely happy.

But something unpredictably sad happened during my packing process, which I shared with these special friends:

"Last night, I wanted to iron my white slacks to put creases in them for the trip. I decided to see what else was in the ironing basket that I hadn't touched in a couple of years. Four of Waverly's shirts were there, and so I starched and ironed them, put them on hangers, brought them to his closet, and then broke down while hanging them up next to the other clothes that I still have.

I don't know if it was a mistake to do that, but I reasoned that even if I gave them away, I would have first ironed them. Still, I sat on his closet floor, picturing us together at the many occasions where he wore each of those shirts. I caught a whiff of his favorite cologne, which lingered in the air.

This morning, I was back to being excited about the trip, so all is well again. You know, I used to be afraid of roller coasters, but no more."

While on the cruise, we all dressed up for dinner each night, which was a lot of fun. As my cabin mate helped me put on my pearls, and strapped me into my high heels, just one tear welled up in each eye. I had always called upon Waverly to change my necklace or bracelet, zip my dress, or buckle my fancy shoes, since I couldn't reach them. Now, when I'm home alone, I must either call a neighbor to assist, or wait until I arrive at my destination to have someone finish dressing me. A sad fact, but not sad enough to make me cry!

At my semi-annual physical checkup in August, the third without Waverly and I going together, the doctor read the results of my blood work. I was in excellent health except for the need to lose weight. However, he strongly suggested that I be checked for eye disease, now that I'm OLDER.

That turned out to be wise counsel because I had something called "narrow angle closure," which is an uncommon form of glaucoma where the iris presses against "something" and prevents the flow of fluids normally. The eye specialist said, *"It's like a dam, and without the release of the pressure, it could sever your optic nerve and cause blindness."* He had my full attention. *"The good news is that laser surgery in the form of an*

Iridotomy will take care of the problem."

Waverly and I had always seen our doctors together, gone to the dentist together, had colonoscopies at the same time! This was my first medical issue, albeit minor, where he wouldn't be with me. My daughter was a phone call away, and my pastor brought me, waited for me, and drove me home since my vision was temporarily too blurred to drive.

I wore sunglasses, but kept my eyes closed during the car ride because light hurt. I felt like you do when you eat ice cream too fast and get a head freeze, but the ache lasted all evening. I couldn't do any reading or writing, so Lucky and I sat on the couch in the dark watching an old movie with Humphrey Bogart and Lauren Bacall, called *The Big Sleep*. I looked like a Hippie wearing short pajamas and sunglasses while sitting in a dark house watching a black and white TV. It marked another "first" without my mate by my side.

During two book signings in Virginia, I met my first (and only) "gentleman caller" as a widow. I was in the Author's Pavilion at a fair in the woods. The tall trees flanked a makeshift stage where my host spoke about this being a celebration of African-American Heritage. Food and crafts vendors participated, and I was the lone author.

An eighty-eight–year-old widowed man, who must have been a good-looking youth, approached me about my book and gave me a big hug. He commented that I felt good, but I chose to make small talk instead of awkwardly responding to the compliment.

When I got back home to Florida, the gentleman called to say he was in bed, but not asleep. *"I was thinking about you and decided to see what you were doing."* The time was 8:20 p.m. He asked if I might want to return to Virginia to spend some time with him, and he offered to purchase a plane ticket for me.

I gently declined, but was flattered when pondering one aspect of my future. It had been a year since my husband passed away, and though I wasn't looking for a companion, I told myself, *"You've still got it!"*

That started my mind thinking about my future as a single woman. Waverly and I were considered by many to be the "alpha" couple. We were always together. When we were dining out, we began counting the guests in our party with the number "2." When we were on vacation with others, the first private sleeping accommodation belonged to the "2" of us!

We never knew how it felt to be the odd number, or the one sleeping on the pull out couch because single people didn't warrant the privacy that couples enjoyed. It was another "first" for me, a new feeling that made me uneasy because it had no parameters.

How would I react if a man close to my age were interested in my company? Could I ever crave companionship enough to engage in a serious relationship with him? How would I reconcile that with my unending love for Waverly? The topic was too far from my present reality to speculate about. I am complete right now, giving my full attention to a tribute to my one true love.

It was September again! Time had flown by over the last few months. I had finished a summer encompassing more travel than I experienced the previous two years. Three social visits and four book signings kept me very busy. I attributed the social visits to Waverly dying. At one time or another, we've all said to distant, but important friends or relatives that we MUST get together someday. Yet we never actually made plans to make it happen.

I resolved that life was too short not to make the effort to share face-to-face time with persons whom I valued. So I contacted three of them, set dates for me to visit, and made travel arrangements. I can't adequately describe the pure joy I experienced by putting forth the effort to follow the Nike slogan – *"Just Do It."*

I end this chapter on getting through the "firsts," with some more profound and gracious words from the famous Helen Keller:

"Walking with a friend in the dark is better than
walking alone in the light."

It's a powerful message to all who are helping someone who is grieving. If you can remember that there is no timetable for grief, and that you can expect to witness a wide range of emotions from the grieving person whom you love, then you will keep supporting, encouraging, listening and empathizing, until you notice raw pain turning towards fond memories. That will be your assurance that WE will eventually be all right.

Chapter Nine
Diet and Exercise
"Give me more...."

For at least three decades, Waverly and I were overweight. We were happy, but heavy. Neither of us was sloppy, and dressing impeccably all the time kept us looking classy wherever we went. At least a year before he died, we talked about "overcoming the last great challenge" in our lives through diet and exercise.

We had a habit of sitting on the gym equipment in the garage and using the stationery bike seat to hold our breakfast tray of a full meal, plus pastries and coffee. We'd watch the birds, squirrels and butterflies within our view, and eat. Then I stacked the empty dishes and carried the tray into the kitchen, with Waverly following me so we could watch morning news. The walk to and from the garage was the extent of our physical activity.

A year ago, we decided to use the equipment for its intended purpose, and each of us had lost *some* weight. We planned to work on the exercise part of our new routine, and gradually add the healthy diet. In the meantime, we consciously split the *Panera* pastries in half, rather than eating two of those big, tasty treats at one sitting. That was enough sacrifice for the first step.

During the seven weeks when Waverly was under his cardiologist's care, we ate fruits and vegetables, decreased carbs and sugars, ate nothing after 7:00 p.m., and were miserable! We did, however, find satisfaction stepping on the bathroom scale, which gave encouraging readings every time we weighed in.

When I found myself reflecting on each spoken word and action between us those last hours before he died, I wondered if Waverly could have lived longer if he weighed less. If so, why had we not gotten the memo? As strong and successful as we were in our marriage and careers, how could we have lacked the willpower to use diet and exercise for longevity? Where did God fit into all of this? I made a commitment right then to diet and exercise for *both* of us, and make him proud posthumously when I accomplished **our goal**.

I had lost almost twenty pounds over the six months before Waverly died, and another ten pounds after that. I was eating healthier and using the treadmill in the garage three times weekly. However, I lacked the discipline to do a full hour of rigorous exercise because I wasn't fond of sweating. It guaranteed me a "bad hair day."

I needed to be in the company of others, taking a grueling exercise class where my pride wouldn't let me stop while everyone else pushed to the end. About that time, I received a coupon in the mail for a free week of exercise and weights at the "Fitness Plus Workout Center." I speculated that this must be a place that existed for us "plus size" women.

I was wrong. The "Plus" stood for every torturous piece of equipment brought forth from Medieval Times, *plus* a number of hour-long classes designed to purge unclean spirits from our bodies through sheer grit and pain. It was my newfound commitment, just three days old, that made me reveal all my personal information to a young, sculpted fitness expert.

The representative measured me *everywhere*, wrote down a bunch of figures on his pad, looked up some things on his master chart, and then spoke his first words to me. *"You have about 44% body fat, which is close to half your weight."* "Yes, I understand what 44% means in all contexts. So what amount of body fat **should** I have?" He replied, *"31% is ideal for women your age and height."* Wow! Only 13% of my whole body needed to disappear for me to be the "ideal woman for my age and height."

"Can you break that down into something measurable for me?" The nice man grinned, then grimaced, then said, *"For optimum health, you should weigh 168 pounds, and I figure it will take two years and a personal trainer to reach that goal."* My eyes moved from viewing his muscular upper body to reading the white letters on his black, tight-fitting tee shirt: "Personal Trainer." What a coincidence that HE was just what he said I needed for the next two years!

He proceeded to tell me that he was a fitness expert who could meet with me for half an hour, twice weekly, for a few hundred dollars a month. I did the math without paper, telling my brain that if my emergency septic tank and my security issues were outside the parameters of my "austerity retirement plan," hiring a personal trainer was definitely out of the question. I gave him a weak smile and looked down at my sneakers.

Losing thirty pounds and two dress sizes within the past year was the miracle of my life, since I had been well over two hundred pounds for three decades. My plan to reward myself when I reached EXACTLY two hundred pounds was to drive around town with my car windows down, blasting the *William Tell Overture* to all within earshot of my boisterous audio display. It mattered not to me whether they understood the reason behind my jamboree. This young man had just burst my bubble!

I elected not to share my plan with the personal trainer, who considered me obese and in need of his help. "So you say my ideal weight should be 168 pounds, eh? Good to know because now I can order a coffin to hold a one hundred, sixty-eight pound woman. When I reach THAT goal, I imagine I'll be ready for burial." He looked confused, which told me I needed to keep my sense of humor to myself when dealing with the leadership at "Fitness Plus."

Instead I said, "I'll skip the personal trainer for now, but I plan to use your machines and take some classes." With that, he abruptly closed his pad and never shared with me my body measurements, nor did he recommend specific exercises. Guess I needed everything everywhere, and clearly I would have to figure out the machines myself, since I had dared to reject the personal trainer idea!

I reviewed the exercise schedule and thought I should do something for my whole body before targeting areas that moved independent of the rest. The first day I met Felix, the Total Body Workout instructor with a gorgeous body and intriguing accent, he asked me in front of the class of anorexic young women if this were my first time coming. What about me caused him to ask that?!

"It's my first exercise class in three decades," I responded, clearing my throat as I spoke. Everyone in the class seemed confident and fit, looking me up and down and making judgments about the new, chubby addition to the class. I looked around and determined that I was the oldest and biggest person in the room. It didn't make me want to run for the door. On the contrary, it made me want to become the "poster child" for "Fitness Plus!"

Everyone had in front of them a stepper, a metal bar with two weights attached to the ends, a set of hand weights, and a round ball, the purpose for which I couldn't fathom! I got all that stuff, and had no problem marching in place to warm up. Then the music started, with a beat that was akin to an express train going past while I spun around like a top on a subway platform.

Losing the rhythm was the least of my worries because as soon as Felix said to lift the bar over our heads and bring it down behind us to touch the base of our necks, both my weights fell off the ends of the silver bar and rolled across the room. A tiny classmate said, *"I help you, Mommy,"* and disappeared in the back of the room. Offended, I wanted to say, "Who you callin' 'Mommy'?" But when she returned with two little grips designed to keep the weights on the bar, I knew that "Mommy" was a term of endearment. No need to explain that I was not a Latina. "Thanks," I said instead. "I thought those little things were female handgrips! Sorry! My bad...."

Felix made certain that everyone understood the meaning of "Total Body Workout" by the end of each class. The only thing more annoying to me than counting backwards and forwards from one to eight several hundred times was holding a position and "pulsing" several dozen more. Towards the end of the second class, Felix came over to me, saying, *"Find your core."* Sweating, with labored breathing, I responded with a pained grin, "My core is sore!"

Driving home from exercise the entire first week of classes was a feat! Do you know how many chest, back, stomach and leg muscles one uses to turn ones' upper body in order to make a lane change? If you've not met Felix, your answer is woefully wrong!

My fourth day of class in three decades would have been horrifying, if I had not passed the age of being horrified. We were standing on the stepper, and the order was given to grab the right ankle and pull the right leg back until our sneaker touched our butt. At the same time, we were to extend the opposing arm and lean forward slightly.

I lacked the balance to even remain on the stepper, but I was determined to keep trying to do the task. I resembled a tightrope walker, despite having a pretty wide platform under my feet. I grabbed the little ankle sock peeking out from the sneaker, surmising that if I could pull the sock behind me, the foot and sneaker would follow. Extending the opposing arm would be a piece of cake after that.

Suddenly, Felix appeared directly in front of me, using his no longer cute accent to shout, *"Give me more!"* Much like the release of a rock from a slingshot, the sock gave way and I lost my grip and my balance, falling into the arms of Felix – literally!! His hard body broke my inevitable fall, nose first, onto the front of the stepper. Only because he had such upper body strength and balance did we not both hit the classroom floor with me on top of him.

Every perfectly poised person in the class remained balanced on one leg, with the other touching their butts. The delicate "flamingo people" glared at their instructor and their infamous classmate. Felix composed himself and moved away from me without a word. Sure my face was red, but the upside was likely that Felix would never again stand close to me saying, *"Give me more!"* I believe I gave him ALL.

The whole thing was my daughter's fault, you know. She said my old white sneakers weighed as much as army boots, and my thick socks that came to my mid-calf looked like war bandages jutting upwards from the heavy sneakers.

For my birthday, she got me a pair of lightweight sneakers with every color of the rainbow on the canvas, in neon, no less! The second gift was a pack of little anklet socks. Had I kept my antiquated, but sturdy sneakers and socks, I would never have fallen into my exercise instructor. Yep, the whole thing was Alicia's fault!

I had two days of using free weights and equipment before Felix held his next Total Body Workout class. I wondered if I should return as if nothing happened, apologize profusely for my clumsy action that might have hurt both of us, play the distressed damsel and say that he was my hero for saving my nose, or give a little wink and smile as I readied myself for the next class. There was also the option of never returning, which might have been Felix's choice for a resolution.

I elected to get to the next class early and have my mat, stepper, weights, ball and bar all ready when Felix arrived. As I approached the big glass window separating the exercise area from the lobby, I stiffened and my heart beat faster as I thought there might be a note on the door saying, "Do not enter," with my picture below the words.

To my surprise, the first three thin classmates to see me ran to get pieces of my equipment for me, and placed them beside me. Was it pity or compassion? I didn't care because it appeared that I had gained the respect afforded a new thug asserting his power on a dangerous street. Oh, he was feared, but the neighbors couldn't do enough to appease him.

I was full of confidence before Felix entered the room and greeted the class. However, when I saw him, my confidence disappeared, replaced by a hint of panic. He scanned the room, no doubt looking for *me*. When our eyes met, he said with a false smile, *"You're back!"* I smiled graciously, thinking to myself, "If he only knew that I have three siblings living in Central Florida who belong to the same fitness chain, it could affect his emotional well-being."

That day, we worked a cluster of muscles, and, despite breathing hard, my body contortions looked *close* to those of my classmates. Then we were asked to lie on our backs on the mats, lean on our elbows, thrust our pelvis towards Heaven, and pulse up and down without allowing our butts to touch the mat.

Finally something I could do well! I wasn't always a widow, you know. I didn't miss a beat. Felix came right to me, looked down and said, *"You are SO there!"* Yes, I WAS so there!! The lyrics to the song he chose for that segment were, *"I want dat boom-boom-boom….Gimmie some a dat boom-boom- boom."* Appropriate!

Feeling smug as I drove home, I sensed both of my elbows were burning. I reached for the elbow of the arm holding the steering wheel, and felt a scrape and small patch of blood. I must have been so determined to do that one exercise to the bitter end that I didn't feel my elbows rubbing against the mat until they bled. I added the elbow pain to the "total body" pain and kept driving!!

I continued to take the Total Body Workout class three times weekly, once in awhile adding a day when I worked with weights and machines. I cheated on my healthy diet about three times weekly, too, but lost weight anyway. The "Exercise Nazi" had my concentrated attention, as I actually improved my coordination and physical capabilities.

Thereafter, when I missed Waverly enough to cry myself to sleep, I tried to focus on Felix as the antidote for grief. Stuck in my mind were sentences like, *"Get into your core." "Focus." "Don't forget to breathe." "Some of you are cheating." "Don't stop, let it burn."* I was concentrating on doing so many bodily contortions at one time that breathing was the last thing I cared about. What was he talking about anyway? How could I exercise **and** breathe?

I attended exercises classes regularly, and saw my stamina and proficiency with the equipment increase. I didn't say I could grab my right knee and push it backwards so I could grab that ankle and pull it securely behind me. I didn't say I could do this maneuver balancing my weight on the stepper and extending the opposing arm while leaning forward slightly. No, I didn't say I mastered that yet!

I was, however, getting better at sitting on the edge of the stepper, keeping my knees *almost* together, back straight, and lifting weights above my head in patterns of eight counts. My initial thought was that Felix should be satisfied that my thighs were inseparable. Being seated and keeping my knees together tightly enough to hold a butter knife between them was a feat for next year. And putting that colored ball between my legs helped not at all! It kept falling and rolling away from me, and I kept chasing it around the room to put it back in place between those unwilling thighs.

After Felix's class one particular day, a class that was preceded by eating and drinking while I was out of town doing book signings and NO exercise, I was feeling sore all over. Even my armpits were telling me not to raise them above my head in the shower. At least most of me could get clean! Washing my armpits was overrated anyway! Had I lost any percentage of my body fat? Only the personal trainer could answer that question, and he wasn't talking!

On another day of exercise class, the sun was particularly bright coming through the window near the high ceiling of the room. In front of us were the tall mirrors, probably to inspire our workout while *some* of us looked at every body dimple. I saw sunlight peeking through the thighs of almost everyone in the room, except me of course.

My shape looked more like the moon, with sunlight affording more of a silhouette than a direct path between my legs. Just then, I spotted sunlight on my body, too, moving through the space just above my ankles. Hey, it was a start!

Felix had a habit of working one set of muscles until his students, one by one, stopped pushing, pulling, squatting or rotating a limb in surrender. After calling out *"Eight, seven…..one"* a full dozen times, he'd say, *"…three, two, one, I LIED, eight, seven…."* There was something sadistic about that man!

After three months of faithfully exercising, despite cheating on my eating during the week, I noticed a visible difference in my appearance. My arms and thighs no longer jiggled, but looked firmer, smoother. I gave an incredulous look into the bathroom mirror, when I recognized my collarbone and chin line, both of which had been barely visible for years!

One morning, as I was getting out of bed, my hand stretched across my butt. Could that be *my* firm derriere? Where had all the dimples gone? When did I acquire butt cheeks able to resist gravity? That left the future task of acquiring a waistline and flat stomach as my "final frontier."

I was pleased enough with my naked appearance to stare at me in the full-length mirror for close to thirty seconds. I could honestly say that I was changing, inside and out, and that I was keeping my promise to lose weight for both Waverly and me! I wasn't, however, ready to think more fondly of Felix than his being my "Exercise Nazi"!

Interestingly, I recalled something I had heard from the Spiritual Care Chaplains during Grief Counseling. *"Exercise releases chemicals to promote a feeling of well-being. It allows muscles to strengthen and relax, which gives you better sleep."* They were making suggestions to the Grief Girls about using physical activity as part of the total healing process. They were right!

I lost two dress and pant sizes, too! The next time I scheduled an appointment with my doctor for a checkup, I smiled as I stepped on the scale. I used to first ask the receptionist to wait until I took my heavy jewelry off, and to find me some nail polish remover before I weighed in. When I updated my health information, asking if I had experienced a number of symptoms since my last checkup, I put a mark next to "weight loss," adding "by design"!!

As Chairman of the Board of a Community Center dedicated to bringing fine and performing arts to under-served children and families, I was a key figure in producing a big fundraising Gala. I had my outfit all picked out – white dress slacks and matching top with a knit white jacket that had silver threads throughout. I chose four-inch high silver, glitter pumps with a t-strap, and a glittery purse to match.

Two days before the event, I tried on the outfit to see if I needed to have it dry cleaned. The slacks barely hung on my hips and looked like I was wearing a sack of produce. If I tugged at them just a little bit, they fell to the floor. Oh, No!

I went to four stores, looking for white dress slacks. It was fall, so there was nothing. Suddenly, I remembered that one of my Grief Girls was accomplished at sewing, painting, weaving, crocheting, planting and much more. I called her in a panic, asking if she might alter my slacks.

Within the hour, I was wearing her much-too-small bathrobe, and she was taking in each pant leg and lining 2.5 inches!! I had worn those slacks less than a year earlier on a vacation with my best friends from college. When she finished altering the slacks, she pressed them for me. I insisted on paying for her exceptional service, but she replied, *"Grief Girls accept no payment for doing something for someone we love. Now get out of here and bring me a picture of you, all dressed up!"*

At the very next Total Body Workout class, I heard the command to lie on the floor, on my back, with legs in the air. We were going to work on upper and lower abs, which I needed badly. Well, my legs felt too heavy to stay straight up in the air, even while wearing those lightweight, neon sneakers. So I crossed my legs at the ankles to keep from dropping them to the floor with a thud.

Felix came around and pushed my knees together without chastising me for the crossed ankles. "I don't think my knees are supposed to stay together, Felix." *"Oh, yes they are, dear lady, so I'm going to stand here and press them together for you while you raise your head and shoulders. Try to bring your nose to your knee, above you."*

Did he say, *"Try to bring my nose to my knee, above me?"* I was doing well to see my fingertips touch my knees, *above* me. My nose was entirely too far away to greet my knees in *this* lifetime! I gave Felix a slight grin, while I gasped for air and saw my whole lower body shake, *above* me. I wasn't sure if I deserved praise for nearly sinking my nose into the fleshy part of my stomach above the navel. After all, it was at least a third of the way to those knees!

Felix noticed me puffing like a blowfish out of water, and he took pity upon me by releasing my knees from the torturous hold into which he had put them. Mercifully, he left me to change the CD.

When the pounding music ended abruptly, there was a moment of silence before Felix reached the stereo and started another loud CD. Someone in the class farted while straining her abs. It *wasn't* me!! All I did was tremble from my waist to the tip of my toes while sporting a natural line of blush for the cheeks (I'm talking about face cheeks, *face cheeks!*).

My legs weren't the only part of my body that trembled. One class featured a lengthy segment of exercises Felix called, "killer abs." That needs no explanation, other than to recount how both my upper and lower stomach muscles danced in unison and in discord, as I rested my entire body weight on my butt with arms and legs outstretched like a pair of open scissors. I believe this was called "getting into my core." I hated the core! I hated hearing my barbarous instructor look in my direction, chanting, *"If it burns, let it burn."* He was void of compassion, that's for sure.

Our session ended right after that, and we quickly put our equipment away and left. After stretching those awful abdomen muscles and working the outer and inner thighs, I walked to my car looking like a toddler with a full diaper – proud of myself, but in need of immediate attention! How could I reasonably be expected to drive myself home after completing that hour-long workout class?

At home, I kept free weights nearby, so that I could multi-task while watching the little bit of television I allowed myself to enjoy. Even when I talked on the phone, I grabbed a weight and pumped it up and down a few times to give me firmer arms by the time I ended each conversation. Waverly would be so proud if he could see me now!

Multi-tasking had its down side, though. I remember getting a phone call one morning, while I was putting on my panties. They ended up sideways, with one leg experiencing constricted circulation while the other didn't know I had underwear on at all. It was mid-morning before I discovered the problem and put them on correctly.

Then there was the day where I had the preparation of breakfast for Lucky and me in a kind of rhythmic pattern. I put her wet kibble in the microwave to warm it, took that out and put my coffee cup with cold milk in to warm it. I had a cup of yogurt and a spoon on the counter, and periodically I sucked down a spoonful of yogurt, as I added dry, crunchy kibble to Lucky's wet food.

Can you guess where this story is going? Yep, I picked up the kibble spoon, mistaking it for the yogurt spoon, and put it deep into my mouth. Ugh! It was time for me to resort to "single jump rope," not "double dutch." I rinsed my mouth more than a few times, talking myself out of throwing up. After all, it was a quality dog food product, just something my taste buds had never experienced. I no longer wanted yogurt that morning, either.

Every time I reached the parking lot of Fitness Plus, I drove up and down a few rows of cars, looking for an open spot. My lucky day came at last, when I found a parking spot only fifty-two steps from the building. It was an end spot next to a concrete curb and a tree that provided shade over my car. Living in Florida means your first choice in seeking parking is to be near shade. Distance from your destination is the secondary consideration.

I briskly walked my fifty-two steps, checked in at the front desk, and had a great class with Felix and my skinny comrades. However, when I returned to the end spot with the tree, my car was gone! I always locked it, and I was holding the keys in my hand. The inside locks were recessed, so no one could unlock it with a coat hanger pushed through the driver's side window.

My heart raced faster than during the whole hour of exercise, just as I saw a state trooper drive past me. God must have sent him. I blurted out the make and model and color of my Audi Q7, scanning the whole parking lot while talking to the trooper. *"Are you sure this is where you parked, Ma'am? Sometimes people think they parked in one place, but actually parked in another. Would you like me to drive you around the Fitness Plus lot, in case you see your car?"*

I gave the trooper a harsh stare, as I affirmed that I had parked where I said I did. A local policeman drove up. The trooper had called him. By now, some folks from the exercise class had gathered around me, offering to take me home or allowing me to use their phone to call someone other than the police.

Through much simultaneous chatter, the local policeman took my statement, and the state trooper left. Two minutes later, he returned, asking me to get in his car so he could drive me to mine. No way was my car in that parking lot!!

Sure enough, I must have taken fifty-two steps in a different direction, where there was a different corner parking spot with a concrete curb and a different tree providing shade. I took a hard look at the whole parking lot at Fitness Plus, suddenly discovering that there were numerous corner parking spots with concrete curbs and trees providing shade to parked cars.

My face turned redder than it looked when I finished the exercise class. It was a false alarm. Both officers were incredibly patient with me, as I stumbled over my words, trying to make amends. I couldn't find enough ways to apologize for the error. I was mortified. I never had anything like this happen to me before, which is why I was absolutely certain that I had made no mistake about where I parked. Now, I just looked absolutely foolish!

Two women from Felix's class stayed with me until I got in my car and drove away. No longer did I view them as thin exercise competitors who out-shined me during every class. They were compassionate women who shared my anxiety, maybe even my embarrassment when the car was located.

As soon as I walked into the room for the next exercise class, nearly all forty persons surrounded me, asking if the police had found my car yet. The rumor about my stolen car reached every ear, so now I had to repeat my confession two dozen times. It was awful!

I didn't think there were degrees of embarrassment and humiliation. However, by the last time I shared the fact that it was I who didn't remember where I parked my car at Fitness Plus, I felt as though I should hide under the stepper instead of standing on it. That's because the last inquirer was Felix! I have no words to describe his facial expression when I revealed that my car was never stolen.

I read the faces of my classmates though: *"Poor dear, she's old and heavy **and** senile,"* to which I responded with my eyes, "If you young things are blessed with increased age and wisdom AND CONFIDENCE like I possess, you'll become ME sooner than you imagined!!" I chose to interpret their pitying looks as concern for their fellow exercise friend. My self-esteem was on the rise again!

The takeaway from losing the car that wasn't stolen, incorrectly putting on my underwear, and spooning dog food instead of yogurt into my mouth, was simple! My cognitive abilities were diminishing in direct proportion to my smaller body size! If things kept going that way, I would become a gorgeous, one hundred and sixty-eight pound imbecile with no body fat, blindly looking for a fitted coffin!!

I reminded myself that my original objective was to lose weight and have better health, for both Waverly's and my sake. An old saying crossed my mind, but I can't recall the author: *"When you're up to your ass in alligators, it's difficult to remember that your initial objective was to drain the swamp!"*

Chapter Ten
I Got a New Attitude
Busy, Busy, Busy with Life

"...Somehow the wires got crossed,
The tables were turned,
Never knew I had such a lesson to learn.

I'm feelin' good from my head to my shoes,
Know where I'm goin' and I know what to do.
I tidied up my point of view,
I got a new attitude.

I'm in control, my worries are few.
'Cause I got love like I never knew.
I tidied up my point of view,
I got a new attitude.

Oo, oo, oo, oo, ooooo,
I got a new attitude!"

Singer, Patti LaBelle

I can't say that I'm fully engrossed in a "new normal" way of living, but I can report with assurance that "I've got a new attitude."

I forgive everyone for everything, and ask everyone's forgiveness who I may have wronged. In Grief Counseling, I learned the importance of forgiveness. *"When you choose forgiveness, you break the bonds of hatred and resentment. Forgiveness is a decision to release past hurts, to let life flow. Although it seems to run contrary to human nature, forgiveness is the most natural choice."* (Robert E. Ross, *The Power of Forgiveness*). I agree with this, and I have searched my heart to discover the ease of forgiveness. Life's literally too short not to do that!

My circle of close friends has grown because of the number of people who loved Waverly so much that they want to be closer to me. My whole family is more tender and attentive than ever, and family get-togethers are important and enjoyable. My best friends offer me constant encouragement and prayer. They never tire of me laying bare my emotions, as I'm fine one day and tearful the next.

I've made some invaluable insights about myself as a new widow. I'm more cautious with strangers and unfamiliar situations because I realize I must handle business as Waverly would. I can't be as overall trusting as I've been all my life, because my personal security depends on my ability to correctly read people and situations. Waverly always took care of that.

I'm physically capable of getting upstairs and downstairs with ease, thanks to my exercise instructor, Felix. Yet I walk down the stairs holding the banister, because if I fall, no one will find me until they realize they can't reach me. I lock all doors, even when going to the mailbox or walking Lucky around our cul-de-sac. I garage my car at night. If I'm writing late at night, I don't wait for bedtime to engage the house alarm. Funny, Waverly used to wish I did any of these things without his prodding. Lessons learned!

How am I managing financially, after my household income was cut in half? As with most young couples, our early years were lean. Waverly and I began our family at twenty years old, before we graduated college and had good paying jobs.

But during all of those decades where we were overweight, productive, successful in our careers and happy, we had plenty of everything. We had a reputation for being extraordinarily generous to all whom we cared about!

For a fleeting moment, I thought I couldn't cope without being able to maintain my existing style of living. The answer for me didn't lie in seeking ways to match yesterday's good living, it relied on my new attitude about the words *"style of living."*

I cut up my ten credit cards, stepping out on faith that I could survive **and** be perfectly satisfied using cash or a debit card. It's made me re-think the definitions of *"want"* and *"need,"* whether I'm shopping or giving. I still occasionally long for *"Waverly's World,"* where pretty much everything I wanted I had. But I quickly reclaim my wandering mind, giving God gracious thanks for all that I have today.

I mentioned my involvement in the local Community Center, bringing arts programs to under-served young people and families. I recall one fundraiser we did, in conjunction with Bloomingdale's. Members of our leadership board volunteered a few hours at the department store, sharing our mission and treating shoppers to some entertainment by our talented kids. A portion of specially identified sales went to the Community Center at the end of the day.

On a break, my body must have been propelled forward in a trance, because I "awoke" in the shoe department, where I used to shop regularly. I reflected on how often I had chosen an expensive pair of shoes, asking if it came in one or two other colors. I silently joked that on my austerity budget, I could purchase one new shoe today, and the one for the other foot in a month.

Truthfully, I still pamper myself and those close to me, but I'm mindful of the difference between *"want"* and *"need."* I make lists of chores and grocery items, not only to be fuel-efficient when running errands, but also to maximize my personal, unencumbered time. I have a large home with more than an acre of property, so I'm now the lady of the house, the cleaning service, the pool service, and a small portion of the landscaping service. Who knew I could juggle all those roles and responsibilities, and be cheerful about it? I absolutely can!

I write things down, keep good records and trust less to memory than to paper and pencil. Yes, I realize I have a computer, too, with a calendar and other applications to make my life easier. The extent of my computer savvy to assist me personally is paying my monthly bills online!

I recently traded my decade-old flip phone that was only good for making and receiving calls, for a modern "LG something" phone that gives me unlimited calling and texting, plus access to the Internet and emails, plus the ability to swipe people's credit cards on my phone when I do book signings. My salesperson at the Sprint store hides when he sees me enter the store to ask another dozen questions about how this new gadget works.

Today, it only takes me seventeen times longer to send a text than to send an email or make a call. However, my "bucket list" includes mastering texting, right after visiting each of the Seven Wonders of the World! I refuse to type acronyms or shorthand for the English language, and I'll never give up using proper punctuation, just because I'm sending a text. On the other hand, I aspire to one day play computer games, phone games, and Facebook games to which I'm always being invited.

Yesterday, my hand slid across the face of the phone, which is very sensitive to touch. Red lines appeared where two of my fingers danced across the screen. I thought I had broken the phone, and rushed to the Sprint store to see if I needed to replace it. Thank goodness I bought the insurance that allows me to get a new phone if something terrible happens to the old one.

My salesperson was taking quick, long strides to get to the back of the store before I called his name, but he wasn't fast enough. He said my phone had a *"scribble"* feature. *"Yeah, you know, in case you want to make notes, you can do it right on the face of your phone."*

I was dumbfounded. "Why would I want to deface my new phone when there's plenty of stationery and writing instruments around me?" I thought I heard him suck his teeth, but I couldn't be sure.

I mentioned how difficult it was for me to not re-live Waverly's last three days, wondering if I could have done something differently, something more that would have kept him with me longer. I believed he would recover, because he showed amazing determination to go upstairs to sleep in the bed with me the two nights he was home from the hospital before he passed away.

So when I knelt in prayer one morning, I found myself yelling at God because I couldn't understand why this man with so much thirst for life with me was taken from me. After I weakly apologized to Him during evening prayers that night, I calmly prayed for discernment. My heart ached and only God could take away that kind of pain.

While I was waiting for the answer to the big question about how long it would take for me to fill the emptiness that hurt to my core, I heard a preacher speak from the *Book of Ruth* in the *HOLY BIBLE.*

The way Ruth handled her personal grief was to leave her people (comfort zone) and venture to a place where she devoted herself to serving her mother-in-law's needs. Through her selflessness, she received God's favor and He replaced her emptiness with purpose and happiness.

God, in fact, had answered MY biggest question, just two months after Waverly died, and in a way I never anticipated. I needed to become more selfless in order to heal myself! What a concept! I happened to be reading the *Book of Luke*, and this appeared before my eyes: **Luke 12:48:** *"…For unto whomsoever much is given, of him shall be much required: and to whom men have committed much, of him they will ask the more."* My mission couldn't have been made clearer, had God spoken from a burning bush on my front lawn!

His immediate plan must have been to put me in situations that forced me to use all of the gifts He had bestowed on me, beginning with my talent for writing. My first novel was inspired by Waverly, and was written in five months as a result of the discipline initiated by Waverly. He chose the only publisher we contacted to read my manuscript, and perhaps it was intended that he would leave me on the day we both discovered that my book would be published.

My first out-of-state book signing was six months after Waverly died, and I was fearful of traveling alone and standing before old friends and neighbors who knew us since we were a young couple. It would be awkward for everyone having to greet me as a widow.

I pushed down the knot in my stomach, established the itinerary, packed my suitcase, made the journey, sold six dozen books, and rekindled relationships with people I should have kept close to me all these years. I even remembered how to be an "Up North" aggressive driver again. I rarely hear a horn blow since moving to Florida, but driving in New York and New Jersey is a *"blood sport."*

My older brother and my best friend were at my side during my first book signing, handing me books, passing me food and water, giving me encouraging smiles, whether I needed them or not.

My former boss' wife, a minister, brought holy oil to bless me and pray with me. I heard many words of praise about the impact I had made on the lives of many of the guests -- things they never told me while I was living near them or working with them.

The only time my anxiety about solo travel returned was when I did a book signing near the town around which I patterned my novel. Some political figures, despicable former parents and unprincipled educators at the school of my last employment felt that some of my fictitious characters resembled them. Pure coincidence!

I made the long drive to another state alone, crying off an on because, during the four years in which I served a school district outside my home state, Waverly did all the driving back and forth monthly. This was my first solo drive, and I wondered if my book signing audience would include unfriendly people. Advertising the event ensured that everyone knew I was coming. Despite some unpleasantness during my two-day stay, I autographed a number of books and returned home without incident.

I've scheduled and attended eight successful book signings since the first, and I can honestly say that I'm comfortable going anywhere, speaking to any audience, sparking old, dear friendships and making new friends along the way. I also built what publishers call *"a platform,"* of about a thousand persons who are interested in my writing. They're anxious to read my second book, as soon as it's published.

I write as often as I can, usually very late at night. But I spend the bulk of most days using my gifts to serve others. I first went to the Community Center at which I'm now Chairman of the Board, to see what a book signing looked like. I had heard that the Center was hosting a few local authors, in celebration of Literacy Month. My plan was to go, observe, and leave ready to serve myself.

God's plan was for me to quickly glean how to do a book signing, after which I would be captivated by the need for voluntary leadership in providing fine and performing arts to children within the impoverished neighborhood surrounding the Community Center. Kids needed a place to explore and showcase their creativity. They needed tutoring to help them realize academic success. The Center needed grant funds to keep the doors open and the programs available.

I began tutoring four high school dropouts interested in earning their GED. I was writing a grant for funding. I was working with the Executive Director to organize a new Leadership Board and establish a yearlong program plan. I paid dues, as a Board member, and pledged additional financial support monthly. It's been such an exhausting and worthwhile endeavor.

Through the process of devoting a good deal of time to this Community Center, I noticed that I cry less often, especially while driving. I ceased to have more than a sporadic restless night, while sleeping well most nights. My appetite improved because I ate more meals with company and fewer alone in my quiet kitchen. I continue to write most of the letters seeking support from, and thanking donors who join me in giving our time, talent and treasure.

Waverly was active in our Homeowner's Association, and close to his untimely death, he was elected to be its secretary. It seemed appropriate to our neighbors that I assume his position.

My logic said that the person with the next highest vote count, or the winner of a special election should assume this coveted position. Nevertheless, I became the Homeowner's Association Secretary, in charge of most correspondences to the neighborhood.

As a result of doing free tutoring at the Community Center, word got around that I tutor students in all subjects and all grade levels. These parents requesting my services *paid* for them, and I had as many as five paid and four free students to teach every week. It was a good balance. I thought God would be pleased!

The one thing all my students had in common, beyond struggling with academic mastery, was self-confidence in their ability to succeed. I did as much to build up their feelings of self-worth as I did teaching the skills they had missed in school. They began to look forward to our weekly tutoring sessions, and so did I.

One little first grader in danger of retention became my client in early fall. She struggled with phonics, math concepts and reading. One day, while she stood next to me as I flashed subtraction cards in front of her, she took a section of my hair and made two long braids next to my ear within seconds.

Once I realized that she liked braiding hair, I offered to let her do anything she wanted to my hair, in exchange for bringing home a perfect grade of 100%. The little girl had never gotten a perfect grade in school – yet.

The next week, this child greeted me with a big hug, pressing into my chest her first perfect paper and exclaiming that she would be giving me a special hairstyle after tutoring. On the table at which we studied together were twenty barrettes and hair clips, each of which tightly held a section of my hair within forty minutes of the end of our tutoring session!

On the way home, I looked at myself in the car mirror and said out loud, *"Waverly, I really need you now, to help me take all this stuff out of my hair!"* The next best option was to stop at my pastor's house, where he and his wife worked tirelessly to remove every barrette from my head. After cutting out a small plug of hair we couldn't save, I was happy to have the rest of my hair returned to me. The child would never forget receiving her first perfect paper, and *neither* would I!

I took pride as a teacher and administrator, in using unconventional methods to get children to discover their gratifying *"ah, ha"* moment. Well, all of my young clients passed their respective grade levels, and I was able to tell myself, *"You're still a 'Master Teacher'."* I was using another God-given talent, but I was also unemployed again!

I mentioned earlier my relationship with The Organ and Tissue Donation Institute, since Waverly was an organ and tissue donor. They called me the day Waverly died, to arrange to take whatever organs could be used to save others' lives. I never expected to hear from them after that.

To my surprise, I received a gift in the mail containing a children's book explaining what might happen when we die, and an embroidered box large enough to hold fifty bereavement cards. The gift helped me organize the cards I'd gotten, and it gave me a way to share with my grandchildren the idea that there's peace and happiness in Heaven when we transition from this life. I was grateful.

Two staff members called shortly after I received the gift, asking how I was doing. Their genuine compassion is what drew me to voluntary service at their establishment. It began with the invitation to visit the Institute, which I'll always remember as the day I learned how to use the GPS in my car.

I joined the Multicultural Committee, co-chaired events honoring both organ donors and transplant recipients, spoke willingly about the benefits of organ and tissue donation, and never missed an opportunity to share my love story with big and small audiences.

Sometimes I participated in Health Fairs, mostly with adults in their work environments. At each fair, someone expressed the fear that if they were critically ill or injured, doctors would let them die if they were organ donors. I learned how to assuage their fears with the undisputable fact that doctors take an oath that their primary duty is to save a life. They would do everything to save the life of an organ donor.

One day, in fifty-nine-degree weather, I was at a middle school, in an open courtyard with winds whipping past all thirteen stations at the fair, where four hundred pre-teens cycled through in groups of three-to-five at a time. The person at the table on one side of me spoke about parks and recreation fun options, and the one on my other side dealt with the dental dangers associated with drinking sweet sodas. Kids readily related to the presenters at both tables, and took the handouts to bring home to their parents.

My topic was organ donation after death. Get the picture? The kids were *seventh graders*, so some giggled as I tried to get them to focus on the fact that many kids, just like them, needed organ transplants. "Young people your age would do anything to jump and play like you do, but they can't," I said, hoping to appeal to their mature side. Did middle school youngsters actually possess a mature side? I knew the answer from having been a middle school administrator.

One girl, of the many wearing designer clothing patterned after the cast of *Les Miserables*, grabbed a boy's shirt, suggesting she was grabbing his heart to donate to the cause. As he attempted to respond with his idea of a *different* organ donation that might interest the young lady, I directed them to the green rubber band bracelets on the table. None of the kids wanted to read the literature, but they eagerly accepted the rubber band bracelets that read, *"Donate Life,"* and they depleted my candy jar with the speed of locusts swarming across a field of grain.

Thank God for the cold Florida weather that particular day, which took my mind off the futility of my situation. I got home, warmed my fingers, and typed an email suggesting to the Organ and Tissue Donation Institute folks that we NEVER AGAIN participate in a middle school health fair, urging pre-teens to discuss with their parents the opportunity to "give the gift of life" when they die!

Recently, I was asked to accompany one of the Institute executives to a state conference on the subject of trauma. It was held at a large hotel on the beach, and there were over three hundred medical professionals in attendance.

As I entered the large ballroom ahead of my time to speak about the human side of organ procurement and distribution, I saw three doctors on stage with a leg and foot from a cadaver. They were operating to repair a major leg break, using clamps and inserting bolts as they talked to the audience. Even though there was no blood to show the audience and me, the sounds of metal pushing against bone were real.

The two large screens on either side of center stage captured the whole thing, enlarging the leg and foot to the size and height of a major league basketball player. The foot was facing ME! I turned toward the refreshment table, where I planned to remain until it was my time to speak.

It's an appropriate cliché to say, *"That's a hard act to follow,"* since we were the next speakers. Two other families had been invited, so there were a total of four speakers representing The Organ and Tissue Donation Institute. The executive staff member presented the sad statistics about the real need for more organ donors. She appealed to these medical professionals to be mindful of these data when dealing with families of deceased patients.

I then spoke about the love and the life associated with a man whose corneas and bones saved someone else's life. I saw a few persons wiping tears as I spoke about my Waverly. I had emotionally connected with this group of medical personnel who were trained to be detached, to some extent, from the death and dying they witnessed daily.

Following me were the parents of a child who received a heart transplant at three months old, and the mother of a young lady who was first a transplant recipient and then an organ donor. Our collective presentation might have been the highlight of the conference, based on the thunderous applause when we left the stage, after announcing that anyone wanting to become and organ donor could go to the national registry at **donatelife.net**.

In addition to being active at the Community Center and The Organ and Tissue Donation Center, I found a professional organization that had spirituality at its core, and business connections after that. The name was *"Simply Sisters Spiritual Professionals,"* and I joined the group at the very first lunch meeting I attended.

It was personally fulfilling to me to see a group of women who only wanted to help each other succeed in business. The conversations were positive, with most members physically and financially supporting all of the other members so that everyone prospered.

It wasn't long before I became an officer in Simply Sisters Spiritual Professionals, and soon after that, I was hosting social events for the group at my home. I enjoyed both the religious and the business connections, and I'm proud to maintain an active presence in this organization.

By now, I had a full calendar of events to occupy my time nearly every day of the week. But God must have felt I hadn't done enough yet to "give myself away." A physician who had supported the students at the school where I was a Florida principal contacted me when he heard I had retired and moved back home permanently. He was still donating time and money to my former school, which warmed my heart.

He asked if I would join the Board of Directors of the institution he founded decades ago called *"Respect Our Earth."* His passion for years had been to heighten people's awareness of the dangers of continuing to pollute and abuse Planet Earth. On numerous occasions, he also brought a team of doctors and other professionals to countries needing clean water systems, new schools, and medical services. The group delivered on its promises, raising required funds from private donations.

How could I refuse to serve on the Board, in addition to supporting this worthy cause, which today impacts every citizen of the Earth? I'm using my grant writing skills to seek out future funding, and my writing abilities to craft correspondences on behalf of *Respect Our Earth.*

We're working hard to ensure the continued success of our annual dinner, fundraiser and auction. The highlight of the annual event is a symposium on climate change, with nationally known presenters giving us the benefit of their documented findings on the subject. There's much to be done for *Respect Our Earth*, and the other impressive Board members join me in relishing the tasks before us.

There's one more initiative in which I'm involved, this one connected to the Community Center. As its sphere of influence expanded to include partnerships with established arts organizations, one of our partners sent us its choir director and half a dozen voices to help start the *"Community Center Gospel Choir."*

As Chairman of the Board at the Community Center, I felt it my duty to show up to the first rehearsal to greet the singers and wish

91

them success. However, before I could say, *"I'm leaving now, but I'll be sitting in the audience at your first concert,"* the director handed me a packet containing five gospel songs to be learned.

I had no intentions of joining the choir. I had no time for the choir. I had no interest in the choir. I stood respectfully, looking for my chance to deposit the packet on the table and escape to my car. After singing three scales of *"la, la, la, la, la, la, la, la, la,"* I was sent to the tenor section! Too late for escape! I sing tenor in the *Community Center Gospel Choir* weekly, thrilled about our first performance in a couple of months.

My daughter, Alicia's reaction to this latest news was, *"See, I'll probably get a visit from Daddy in a dream because I wasn't supposed to leave you alone this long."* I assured her and myself that, *"I ABSOLUTELY WON'T VOLUNTEER TO DO ANOTHER THING – NOT ANOTHER THING! After all, I'm firstly an author with three or four more books to write and publish, correct?"* Alicia didn't respond.

Part of my *"new attitude"* is accepting the freedom that comes from living alone. I focused for a long time on the loneliness and the pain of being without Waverly. Somewhere in my journey to find my *"new normal"* way of living, I felt a liberty I had never known. Couples who are blessed with a long life together don't just finish each other's sentences and know each other's thoughts without using words to express them. They also think and act with their mate's desires and tastes in mind.

I've learned that I can be alone without being lonely. I've begun to experience a kind of freedom from the constraint that goes along with a blissful marriage. I only have to think of myself when choosing what to do, what to eat, with whom to meet each day. That's a brand new sensation for me, having married at age nineteen and been completely satisfied being Waverly's life partner for almost forty-five years. It was he who made all the decisions about where we lived, the cars we drove, and nearly all of the vacations we took over the years.

My daughter, husband, and four grandchildren give me immense joy. I live half an hour from them, and see them often. I'm able to admire Alicia and Bruce's parenting skills as they impart faith, knowledge, patience, gratitude, and respect in their children.

They've taught their children to be kind and studious, willing to complete assignments that take them well beyond the normal school day. They've taught their children how to accept the death of their Grandpa, and later, how to accept the death of a pet. They're heavily invested in the teaching and learning process for their kids.

I recall one Election Day, when the whole family went to the local polling place so the parents could vote. In the waiting area, the children were allowed to read mock ballots and get a sense of the voting process.

As they bubbled in their election choices, one child said aloud, *"Mom, who is Janet Reno?"* The oldest child, almost eleven years old at the time, asked, *"What does 'dem' and 'rep' mean?"* The polling place was relatively quiet, except for my grandchildren. The parents tried in vain to explain the importance of exercising our right to vote, and in the end, they wisely agreed to save this civics lesson for a day when the children were older.

Alicia is home-schooling all four children, while teaching undergraduate classes online. Doing all of that and maintaining a household has helped her master the art of time management! I'm enjoying my child more as an adult than I did when she was a child. And I adored her when she was a child!

My two sisters and I started sending morning emails to each other, and that has morphed into a daily blog among the three of us. Each morning, I delight when I read and respond to the sisters' morning messages. I look forward to reading a scripture sent to me daily by my youngest sister.

I regularly keep in touch with my BFFFFs (Best Friends Forever From Fredonia), and we take trips together more often than we did when Waverly was alive. I schedule time monthly to be with my Grief Girls, and I'm part of another group of special ladies whom we affectionately refer to as the *Girls Night Out Group*.

I have not one, but five husband and wife pastors in my life, including my son-in-law's parents and the couple I consider my "main" pastors. All of these powerful messengers of God have embraced me, comforted me, taught me the meaning of scriptures and prayer, and blessed me with their respective friendships.

One thing I still struggle with is knowing when the time will be right for me to empty Waverly's bedroom closet and drawers. I've given a significant amount of clothing, shoes and accessories away. But there is still half a walk-in closet full of things, and four dresser drawers full of casual and bedroom attire.

I think I fear that once the last articles of Waverly's clothing are gone, he'll disappear. Intellectually, I know that's not true. But emotionally, it's hard for me to accept that when a person dies, all of his or her belongings – those things that identify the person as unique and special – fall away. Never mind that these things can be a blessing to someone still alive and grateful to receive a "piece" of Waverly.

In Grief Counseling, we learned that there is no rush for grieving persons to rid themselves of their loved ones possessions. Eventually, they will part with tangible things in favor of fond memories and pictures. I look forward to the day that happens for me.

In time, I'll find the courage to take that final step to separate me from the articles of Waverly's clothing that have his scent in them. Clothing that is tied to an endless reminder of things we did and places we went together. I still have his favorite cologne on my dresser.

Then, there's all the memorabilia associated with Waverly's love for Black pilots and cowboys, guns and swords, saddle bags, his pipe with some cherry blend tobacco still in it, imported cigars and humidor, and his model cars of BMWs and Corvettes.

Daily, I look at Waverly's stable of seventeen leather horses, the largest of which is four feet tall, with the head facing toward Waverly's side of the bed. I sleep on that side sometimes, and when I wake, I give a nod to the horse on my way to the bathroom.

I'm open to creating new memories every day. Perhaps new memories will eventually give me the strength I need to push aside old things. I'm not just busy to avoid having too much time to grieve. I'm doing what I love, while using all my talents and strengths to the benefit of others.

I still cry during a portion of every week that I'm alive. But I put those tears into perspective, instead of letting them consume me. My pastor's wife hugged me, saying softly that God collects our tears and keeps them in a bottle to show his everlasting concern for us.

Alicia said, *"Mom, you're so busy, you need wardrobe changes."* That's true. Through introspection, I've come to realize that my days are as full and rich as they were when Waverly was with me. They're just filled with different, but equally important activities to which I alone must attend.

I pay attention to the little, wonderful things in my life that used to go unnoticed because I was busy, busy, busy with my career. I make breakfast each morning for Lucky and me, and then take her for a walk. I love the smell of breakfast when I return home.

I spoke about the time when Waverly and I used the exercise equipment in the garage for a table to hold our tray of too much food, drink and dessert. We'd eat and look out at nature, the sounds of which were easy to hear because we weren't breathing heavily from exercising.

Sometimes, we saw the rain come down. Waverly's favorite was a soft rain that covered the entire driveway, and that was accompanied by a gentle breeze. At the Home Going Celebration, there was no rain, but there was a gentle breeze blowing in the back yard throughout the memorial. Today, I look for light rains and gentle breezes, and when I find them I stop whatever I'm doing to appreciate them, in Waverly's honor.

I look at the sky every morning and evening, in awe of the beauty to which God treats every observant eye. I no longer care if it's a bad hair day because it's more precious to me to be alive than to have good-looking hair. I like *Bible Study* because, although I prided myself on having read the *HOLY BIBLE* more than once, I'm only now discovering its true meaning for my life.

In terms of my technology prowess, I know how to change the batteries in my computer mouse and keyboard. I can clean up my desktop by creating folders, play tunes while I work, scan photos and send faxes. I know how to purchase a movie from my television and view it in surround sound. I operate all four stereos in my home now, changing CDs and playing DVDs.

With my new Android phone, I can make and receive calls, text *very slowly*, use the Internet and check emails. The other ninety features are mine to learn another day! The important thing is that I *have* moved into *this* Century!

I'm pretty good at maintaining my Audi Q7, though I'm coaxed by computer messages telling me what to do and when to do it. For a couple of months now, I haven't seen an exclamation mark after reading a command to service the car or rotate the tires or refuel. I have earned the respect of the vehicle.

I also have the whole home security thing down well, too. I'm not afraid of the dark or the noise in the night. I still can't work the intercom system, but I haven't set the alarm to go off in the middle of the night either. I'm excellent at keeping the pool clean and ready for swimmers, if I do say so myself.

The bottom line is that I always *could* be more independent, but I didn't have to until Waverly died. I've always been confident in my abilities, and fearless in my refusal to compromise my integrity for any superficial reward.

I believe I'll know when the time is right to move from this large home to a smaller dwelling. Right now, living here gives me serenity because this is where Waverly left me. I'm meeting my financial obligations, and I travel to see the people I love most, while all of us are still alive. I treasure all of my relationships as the most valuable gifts that I possess.

I shared my first dream about Waverly appearing and embracing me with a slight smile. I only saw his upper body and face before he disappeared from my arms. Even though I initially awoke to a warm feeling of having felt his affection and protection, I cried hard when I concentrated on Waverly's firm embrace in the dream. I felt safe and cared for all the time, and waking was a stark reminder that my secure feeling was gone.

Since that first dream, I've had four more to date. I haven't a clue how to interpret them, singly or together, but every time I awoke from a dream about Waverly, I felt peace.

Waverly wore glasses most of his adult life. In my second dream, his glasses were falling slowly on an angle under water, until they sank to the ocean floor. I neither saw nor heard him, but I immediately recognized those gold rim glasses. The water was blue and calm, and I saw the glasses clearly, even when they hit the bottom.

My third dream was of me in my present home, walking by the French doors to the lanai. The doors were closed, but I glanced outside to see Waverly walk from left to right, with a tray of food to cook on the grill for guests who were gathered outside. He didn't glance my way, but I wasn't concerned because I would join him when I finished whatever I was doing. My task remained undefined throughout the dream, and I never got to join Waverly before I woke up.

The fourth dream was hearing his brisk walk as a younger man, coming down the steps of our previous home to answer the door and handle some matter at hand. I sat in the living room, waiting for him to return and tell me what happened. Whatever transpired at the door was not combative because I heard no sound beyond mumbling. I awoke before Waverly could return to me with news.

In my fifth and last dream, I was in that sleep state where you're just about to wake up. Waverly and I were huddled close together on the floor of a ship, which was making a sharp counter-clockwise turn. As we rocked back and forth, he gently pushed my head in his breast and put his hands over my eyes and cheeks.

He knew I was prone to dizziness, even riding a Ferris wheel. I wasn't alarmed because I felt completely shielded from harm while in his bosom. I knew everything would be OK once the turn was completed and we could get up from the floor. Then I awoke, holding my pillow tightly.

I'm *learning* to listen to music without relating the songs I used to love to the loss of my life's mate. Within the next year, I imagine I'll part with the rest of Waverly's clothing, accessories and "man cave toys," preferring instead to savor the memories associated with those tangible items.

I sense that Waverly is genuinely proud of the way I'm carrying on without him, but I would go to sleep right away, if I thought he would visit me and speak the words that assured me I was on the right path to fulfill my destiny. Perhaps only God can give me that assurance, but He hasn't been much more talkative than Waverly!!

I heard a television evangelist say, *"It's not what you gather, but what you scatter that tells what kind of life you have lived."* I feel secure in the knowledge that I've scattered many good seeds over my career in education. However, the seeds I'm scattering since being on my own seem more precious as they leave my hands to drop into the rich soil beneath my feet.

Maya Angelou – *"Stand up straight and realize who you are, that you tower over your circumstances. You are a child of God. Stand up straight."*

Only once did I ask God to show me a sign that He didn't make a mistake in taking Waverly exactly when He did. I agonized one full night wondering if Waverly were selfless enough to move out of the way to make room for me to blossom as an independent being. Or, had Waverly accomplished all that God wanted from him, and it was time to call him home? Or, had Waverly's positive spirit about getting well weakened for the briefest moment, after which it was too late to remain in this world?

It was at the end of that long, tearful, sleepless night that I turned in my *HOLY BIBLE* to this, the answer God waited until morning to reveal because I was finally ready to accept it:

Ecclesiastes 3:1-8:

"To every thing there is a season, and a time to every purpose under the heaven:
A time to be born, and a time to die; a time to plant, and a time to pluck up that which is planted;
A time to kill, and a time to heal; a time to break down, and a time to build up;
A time to weep, and a time to laugh; a time to mourn, and a time to dance;
A time to cast away stones, and a time to gather stones together; a time to embrace, and a time to refrain from embracing;
A time to get, and a time to lose; a time to keep, and a time to cast away;
A time to rend, and a time to sew; a time to keep silence, and a time to speak;
A time to love, and a time to hate; a time of war, and a time of peace."

So, what's the next chapter in my life? As I proofed this manuscript, I discovered that, as my spiritual walk took shape during the grieving process, I interjected an increasing number of Biblical scriptures that carried me forward. I hadn't noticed that while I was writing the book, but in retrospect, I perceive that they gave me purpose and direction during times when I felt worried, confused, helpless, even hopeless.

My heart's desires are to strengthen my faith, digest the HOLY BIBLE, and continue to share my talents in every way possible. I remember in one of the Grief Counseling sessions that the Spiritual Care Chaplains reminded us that WE didn't die, and we needed to choose for ourselves a path to a fulfilling life. My "new normal" begins with God.

I live by these simple words from another of my Grief Counseling sessions: *"Time heals almost everything. Give time time. No matter how you feel, get up, dress up and show up every single day!"* When I do this, I *always* find someone who needs something from me, and whose need is greater than mine. That discovery puts into perspective any thoughts of self-pity or envious quest that might have crept into my heart while I slept.

I felt that God's hand was in my first novel, HOODLESS KLAN, because every time I sat at the computer to write, the words flowed from my fingers with almost no corrections. I never experienced what they call "writer's block!" I wrote until I had nothing more to say. That book was the biggest one my publisher had ever printed and bound.

FINDING HUMOR IN GRIEF is very different, shorter, with all the characters and actions centering around my beloved Waverly's life and death. There's far more humor than grief described here, which is exactly what God provided to me since I became a widow -- more laughter than hurt.

I wrote my last pages from sundown one day to nearly dawn of the next, feeling exhilarated that the work was completed. But I was astonished when I awoke crying. The empty sensation began while I brushed my teeth and dressed, and didn't leave me until late afternoon.

Was it due to my relief that this tribute was finished? Was it satisfaction over the anticipation of a publication date soon? Or was this just like the understandable feeling of diminishment I got when I finished putting together Waverly's quilt square for the organ donation mural?

Then I remembered something else from Grief Counseling. We read a piece from Marcia Alig's *Up, Up and Away: Practicing the Art of*

Letting Go. "One of the aspects of letting go...is the idea that it is the final act of the grief process. We may feel that it is a denial of our love." On the contrary, it's a validation of our complete loyalty to the person whom we love deeply. Letting go is not only cathartic for the person grieving, but some say it is necessary for the spirit of the deceased to find permanent rest.

THAT'S what was in my mind, gnawing at my heart until I felt depressed enough to spend most of the day in my home crying. I was unable to name it, but I was anxious about closing the "chapter" of my life devoted to sharing my journey through the first years of grief. I'll never deny my love for the only man I've ever known – likely the only one I'll ever know!

"In letting go, we allow our love to free itself from the painful memories linked with death, and thereby we affirm our everlasting love." Therefore, after consciously putting God first in my life, I'm letting go as fast as my intellect and heart will allow. I needed to affirm that by finishing this book, I wasn't abandoning Waverly's precious memory, but rather intensifying it!

My sister's pastor sent this beautiful message about transitioning from life on earth to life everlasting:

"Ripe fruits of choice experience are gathered as the rare repast of life's evening, and the soul prepares itself for rest. The Lord's people shall also enjoy light in the hour of death. Unbelief laments; the shadows fall, the night is coming, and existence is ending.

Ah, No, crieth faith, the night is far spent, the true day is at hand. Light is come, the light of immortality, the light of a Father's countenance. Gather up thy feet in the bed, see the waiting bands of spirits! Angels waft thee away. Farewell, beloved one, thou art gone, thou wavest thine hand.

Ah, now it is light. The pearly gates are open, the golden streets shine in the jasper light. We cover our eyes, but thou beholdest the unseen; adieu, brother, thou hast light at even-tide, such as we have not yet."

THE END

References

Black Eyed Peas. (2009). Boom Boom Pow [Recorded by Black Eyed Peas]. On *Boom Boom Pow*. United States of America:

Interscope Records.
Blevins, T., J.D. (2012). EarthWeb Foundation, Inc. www.earthwebfdn.org.

Crowe, C. (Producer), & Crowe, C. (Director). (2011). *We Bought A Zoo* [Motion Picture]. United States of America: 20th Century Fox.

Dobbs Funeral Home. West Orlando Chapel. (2012). Orlando, Florida. Testimonials on website www.dobbsfuneralhome.com.

Hunt, B. (Director), JLT Productions. (2000). *Return to Me* [Motion Picture]. United States of America: Metro Goldwyn-Mayer.

Kimbrough, M. CEO/Executive Director. (2012). Shine Pine Hills Community Performing Arts Center. Orlando, Florida. www.pinehillsperforms.org.

Pitts, M. (2012). Business Women's Inspirational Network (BWIN), Orlando. Florida. www.BwinInc.com.

Plumley, Rev. M., MDiv, BCC. Chaplain/Supervisor. (2012). Dr. Phillips Hospital, Spiritual Care Department, A Journey Through Grief.

Robinson, S. (1985). New Attitude [Recorded by Patti LaBelle]. On *New Attitude*. United States of America: MCA.

Scripture quotations taken from the *Holy Bible*, King James Version®, © 1988 by Thomas Nelson, Inc.

Sims, T. (2005). You Will [Recorded by CeCe Winans]. On *Purified*. United States of America: Puresprings Gospel, Epic Records.

TransLife Organ/Tissue Donation Services. (2012). Winter Park, Florida. www.Translife.org.

Vandross, L., and Marx, R. (2003). Dance with My Father [Recorded by Luther Vandross]. On *Dance with My Father*. United States of America: J Records.

Postscript
Written Tributes to
Waverly Lee Baskerville, Jr.
(chosen from among one hundred online posts and cards)

He was born in South Hill, VA, where he lived until age seven, when he and his family moved to Newark, NJ. He was the eldest of four children, all boys! He accepted the Lord and for years was a member of Mt. Olivet Baptist Church in Newark, NJ.

Waverly went to the State University College at Fredonia, NY, where he met and married Ruth Cheatham months later. Through their union, one child, Alicia, was born while they were still in college. Waverly and Ruth enjoyed each other's company during forty-four years of marriage.

Waverly earned his B.S. and M.B.A., working thirty years for top investment banking firms on Wall Street. He became First Vice President of Salomon Brothers, Inc. He served ten years on the Board of Education in Orange, NJ, and was President the year his daughter, Alicia graduated from high school. That meant that his signature was on her diploma. He was an officer in the Southern Acres Home Owners Association in Windermere, FL before he died. Waverly was an avid collector of cars and African-American memorabilia, particularly Buffalo Soldiers and Black pilots.

His mother, Lydia Belle Baskerville and brother, James Sherman Baskerville preceded him in death. He is survived by wife, Dr. Ruth Baskerville, daughter, Alicia Lankford, son-in-law, Bruce Lankford, father, Waverly Baskerville, Sr., brothers Larry Baskerville and Phillip (Angela) Baskerville, grandchildren, Bruce, Jalyn, Kennedy and Avery Lankford, along with a host of nieces, nephews, in-laws and friends. A memorial service will be held at his home in Windermere, FL on Sunday, March 18, 2012 at 2:00 p.m., and will be officiated by Bishop Richard B. Lankford, Sr., from the Atlanta International Christian Praise Center in Atlanta, GA."

Throughout the years we shared, Waverly always signed his cards to me with the words, "Darling, Forever."

Ruth's post to the funeral website the day after the Home Going Celebration:
"I think part of my morning ritual will be to log onto this website to read and

send comments about my beloved Waverly. Yesterday's celebration was amazing, with perfect weather and breezes that blew at important times throughout the ceremony. Butterflies and birds flew past the gathering, as did the wasps attracted to all of the flowers.

As much as I feel sad, I recognize that I'm the luckiest lady around because of the overwhelming love surrounding me. I knew so many things about my daughter, Alicia, but not how much of an anchor she is in keeping me from ever sinking.

So many took charge of a piece of the program or the meal. My sister-in-law turned our backyard and lanai into an elegant venue for the Home-Going Celebration. My son-in-law brought every kind of technology known to man, to bring Pop Baskerville's reading of **Psalm 125** to Florida from New Jersey. My pastor gave a stirring invocation, and my son-in-law's Dad preached a sermon that sounded like he and Waverly had grown up together as brothers.

It's quiet in the house right now, still dark outside, and overnight guests are sleeping. But I'm not alone. I'm never alone because I feel the presence of God Almighty!"

Daughter, Alicia said, "I will miss you forever, Daddy! Brucie, Jalyn, Kennedy and Avery wanted to say, 'Hi Grandpa! We miss you for sure, but we know that God's got you. Please tell the Angels we said hi.' I can't believe that my Daddy is gone from me. One day, I'll be able to dance with my father again. I love you, Daddy."

Vern-Vern (nickname from Waverly to Alicia), posted on her Daddy's funeral website, "I can't seem to get the word surreal out of my mind! This whole experience has seemed like such an odd dream from which I have been looking extremely forward to waking; yet it never seems to end. Funny, I always thought an unending dream would be something happier and lighter, but this is quite the opposite. My heart aches for a number of reasons and for a number of people, but mostly for my dear Mommy. I love you, Daddy!!"

Richie, Ruth's brother wrote, "My Dear Brother-in-Law, Waverly, You have loved my sister so very much for these past forty-four years, and I will always love you for that. You and Ruthie raised a beautiful daughter whom I am very proud of. You have made them both strong, and they know they will see you again…and so will I. What a blessing that I had you in my life over all these years! You were an inspiration to me and will be missed….until we meet again."

Rachelle, Ruth's baby sister sent these encouraging words right after Waverly's passing: *I Corinthians 15:54-55: "So when this corruptible shall have put on incorruption, and this mortal shall have put on immortality, then shall be brought to pass the saying that is written, Death is swallowed up in victory.*

Oh, death, where is thy sting? O grave, where is thy victory?"

Shirley, Ruth's friend and fellow administrator spoke these words at the Home Going Ceremony: ***John 14:2-3:*** *"In my Father's house there are many mansions. If it were not so, I would have told you. I go to prepare a place for you, and if I go and prepare a place for you, I will come again and receive you to myself, that where I am, there you may be also." "Your Waverly has gone ahead to prepare a space for his beloved wife, whom he shall surely see again one day."*

Tammy and Chris, family members said, *"Ruth, it was a wonderful service and we will never forget Waverly, ever. We'll always look for him at holidays, and will miss his big laughs when we would talk. He was such a wonderful, genuine and real person who will be missed by so many people, and we'll never forget him."*

Andrea, BFFFF from college posted, *"Dearest Waverly, you were so special to so many people. It was my privilege to have known you for 46 years--what a blessing. Make a place for all of us when it is our time. I cannot believe your physical presence is not here anymore. Keep your spirit with all who love you.*

Dearest Ruthie, my love, you found a life partner that filled all your needs, wants, etc. - your helpmate. You were so blessed. I am sorry you won't have him in the physical world, but he will never leave you in spirit. I hope you know all of us who love you are here for you, and will never get tired of hearing you talk about Waverly! I love you and will work on getting to see you in quieter times."

Nicole T., Waverly's Wall Street colleague☐ said, *"Dear Ruth, Your tribute to Waverly is beautiful and perfectly captures his love of life, friends and family. I am lucky to have shared with you and him some of this joy and affection. Waverly, you and your family are in my prayers. I offer my sincerest sympathy. Much love."*

Nicole B., Waverly's Wall Street colleague and mentee expressed her deepest sorrow: *"Dearest Wave, Who would have known when I sat down across from you fifteen years ago for my job interview that I would have gained another father, because that's what you were to me, never just my boss. That interview was more of a conversation.*

Over the years, you, Ruth and Alicia welcomed my husband and I into your family, and we will always treasure the sit-downs we had together. I regret only that we didn't see you more often. I always thought I would have more time with you.

It's taken me four long weeks to put these few thoughts down because I wanted to be able to do so without crying. I'm not doing a very good job of that. Just the thought of your not being around is unfathomable, and I will miss your wise counsel terribly. I can still hear your great booming voice and laughter, and I comfort myself with the thought that you are making heaven a wonderful place and looking out for us down here.

I'll treasure the memories I have of you, and I know I'll see you someday. In the meantime, as we Jamaicans say, 'Walk Good.' I'm your other daughter."

Alexis, Ruth's friend and administrative colleague wrote, *"My heart is truly heavy for you and the family. Know that Archie and I will continue to keep you all in our prayers. Your tribute to Waverly said it all. You have such wonderful and countless memories of your true and unending love. Stay strong, my Sister, because I love you."*

Patti, Waverly's Wall Street colleague and mentee☐ said, *"Dear Waverly, I am such a lucky girl to have met someone like you in 1993 when I joined the Firm. Although we only worked together for a short time, you have helped me in so many ways.*

Thank you so much for being so kind to some Chinese girl who just graduated from college. Thank you for believing in me. You were a great boss, a true friend and the best mentor. I'll always remember everything you taught me, and the great stories you shared with me.

I am so glad we reconnected over the last couple of years and shared some more laughs and stories. Dear Ruth, please take good care of yourself. Waverly will always be watching over you! Hugs and Kisses."

Sarita and Jimmy, close family friends posted, *"Dear Waverly, It was a blessing to have known you. You inspired so many people in your life. Your love lives on in Ruthie, Alicia and family. We know you are in the presence of our Lord! Ruthie, God's love will always surround you. You will never walk alone!* **(Isaiah 60:20:** *Thy sun shall no more go down; neither shall thy moon withdraw itself: for the Lord shall be thine everlasting light, and the days of thy mourning shall be ended.') We are here for you anytime of the day or night."*

Russ, Alicia's friend wrote, *"Waverly was a kind, gentle, man with enormous strength of character. I am fortunate to have had the opportunity to know him and be inspired by his great success in life through hard work, discipline, passion, and love. His boundless love for his family was irrefutable. You are all in my thoughts and prayers."*

Mark, Ruth's educational colleague and dear friend posted, *"Waverly, you were like family to Alexis and me. Your guidance, kindness and* *wisdom will be sorely missed. You helped me find perspective and strength during some dark days in my career. I followed your advice and always came out on top. You were a winner in every sense—a winner as a husband, father, grandfather, uncle, friend, business leader and community leader. You will always have a place in our hearts."*

James P., Ruth's friend wrote, *"My thoughts and prayers are with you, my dear Ruth. Losing a loved one is always difficult, but as I often tell my loved ones and friends, 'We do not know the hour of our arrival, nor do we know the hour of our departure;' that is in the hands of the Almighty because He is the conductor of this train."*

Rodney, former neighbor said, *"So sorry for your loss. I have fond memories of you guys from the neighborhood where Alicia and I grew up. As a child, I remember when Mr. Baskerville got that first Corvette, and he would sit on the front steps and just stare at it in the driveway. I didn't quite understand it until I finally started to achieve some of my dreams as an adult. He will be missed."*

Julius, Waverly's Wall Street colleague and mentee, attached this message to a large gift: *"Waverly was my mentor and hero. Know that my heart is with you during your time of loss. I send deepest sympathy to you and Alicia, Ruth."*

Kathy R., Ruth's friend and organizational leader wrote, *"Dr. Ruth, you are an inspiration to many. You and Waverly were very fortunate to have found each other, and it is a testament to both of your characters, and your love, that you stayed together forever. I know those wonderful memories will keep you company. Much love to you and your family."*

Vanessa, Ruth's oldest friend's daughter said, *"Sending warm, caring thoughts to wrap around your broken heart and keep it safe until you're strong again. I loved Waverly very much. He'll be missed."*

Teresa, Ruth's educational colleague wrote, *"We are so, so sorry for your loss. Waverly was an awesome husband, friend and father. You are so blessed to have been part of each other's lives. My husband remembers what an awesome birthday party he had for you. I hope each time his beautiful face comes into your mind you remember how much he loved, honored and cherished you. Please give our love and respect to Alicia.*

Kathy G., Ruth's educational colleague wrote in a lovely card, *"My* heart was broken when I learned of the sudden death of your dear husband. I had the good fortune to meet him. Such a great man! I offer you my sincere sympathy. Please accept this card and words as warm hugs to wrap yourself in during this difficult time and afterwards."

Emry, Ruth's educational colleague posted, *"Dr. B., You and your family are constantly in my prayers. Waverly was such a strong man who would do anything to protect his family. We will surely see him again. He is in heaven smiling down on us all. Remember, God always picks the prettiest flower first. Love Ya!"*

Willis, service volunteer: *"I was deeply saddened to hear about Waverly. I am so glad you all had some time together during the past several months, and I hope that will provide you with many comforting moments. Some from our organization who have kept in touch with you tell me how well you are handling the situation, and I'm proud of you! I'm keeping you in my prayers for peace and comfort."*

Cathy, Ruth's friend and former boss expressed her condolences: *"I, too thought very highly of you ad Waverly. I always thought you were a well matched and much in love couple. My heart and prayers go out to you and your family. From my experience, only time helps. I know that Waverly's legacy will live on with the family."*

Christopher, Alicia's friend sent a card: *"My family and I are sorry to hear about your loss. Our prayers are with you and your loved ones".*

Ron and Beth, neighbors, sent an arrangement and card, which read: *"We certainly mourn with you and share your sorrow in the loss of Waverly. We love Waverly and will miss him dearly! He was an awesome, intelligent, tenderhearted and encouraging friend and neighbor. Please know that we are continually here to help you in any way, Ruth. We love you."*

Tina, Alicia's friend, sent this message on a gift: *"I am sending you my sincerest condolences. I know the loss is great and no words could make it easier. It was a blessing to know Mr. Baskerville, a great man!*

Yvonne, Ruth's educational colleague said, *"I sincerely am sorry for the loss of your husband. You were there for me through the loss of my son, for which I am and will always be truly grateful. As a matter of fact, you were always supporting my family during hard times. I'm praying for your family now."*

Phil, Waverly's baby brother, posted several messages on the funeral website, and here are four of them. He still finds it incredulous that his big brother is gone, but he takes comfort in knowing he was the last person to share words of encouragement with Waverly about his health.

"To my dear Big Brother, Junior, I'm so thankful that we spoke the way brothers should by telling each other that we love one another! I'm going to miss you forever. I've always been proud of you, Brother. You helped me become the man I am today.

I know you are in a better place, and I'm proud of you because you tried to stay. It's OK, get your rest. Sister will be fine for I got her back for you, Brother. You will always be my Big Brother, until we meet again."

"Today makes three weeks since my dear brother has gone to Glory. I miss him so much, but my memories of him keep me comforted. I was thinking how my big brother was always there for me, from the times he used to come home from college on break, to the time he met his sweet wife. I would protect what was Junior's when he wasn't around. That's how my brother and I took care of each other! Love you brother for all of the good times we shared."

"My dear brother, everything I've been doing lately reminds me of you, from working in the yard, cooking out, watching movies and laughing at each other's corny jokes! I don't have to tell you how much Pop misses you. Sometimes he would say that his namesake is gone! Pop says that he was blessed to have you for a son! He always said you treated him like royalty!

I told you when I called you everyday you were sick that I love you!! I would say to you what Superman said: "That's what I'm here for!!" I love you Junior, you were my best friend, Brother, and I will always be your Li'l Brother."

"Dear brother, I was thinking of you like I always do, and how April was the month I took vacation with the family and spent time with you and Sister in GA. I'm still having problems with that being the last time we saw each other! You were my BFF. I've always been a loner, but you surely were my partner! I'm just feeling a little funky today, but it's OK, this is my healing process.

How to Reach the Author

I hope I've made my readers, whether grieving or helping those who are grieving, laugh a lot and weep a little as they heal! If I can support others who are coping with grief, I invite readers to reach out to me via my contact information below. I'm available for book signings, book club gatherings, open mic/spoken word readings, or intimate conversations with individuals or groups of persons going through grief.

www.ruthbaskerville.com
www.facebook.com/ruth.baskerville.3
www.drruthscorner.blogspot.com
wrbaskerville@aol.com

Made in United States
North Haven, CT
09 April 2022

18079321R00065